second manassas 1862

robert e. lee's greatest victory

JOHN LANGELLIER

second manassas 1862

robert e. lee's greatest victory

Praeger Illustrated Military History Series

Westport, Connecticut
London

Library of Congress Cataloging-in-Publication Data

Langellier, John P. (John Phillip)
    Second Manassas 1862: Robert E. Lee's greatest victory / John Langellier.
       p. cm. – (Praeger illustrated military history, ISSN 1547-206X)
    Originally published: Oxford: Osprey, 2002.
    Includes bibliographical references and index.
    ISBN 0-275-98447-8 (alk. paper)
    1. Bull Run, 2nd Battle of, Va., 1862. I. Title. II. Series.
    E473.77.L36   2004
    973.7'32–dc22   2004050382

British Library Cataloguing in Publication Data is available.

First published in paperback in 2002 by Osprey Publishing Limited, Elms Court,
Chapel Way, Botley, Oxford OX2 9LP. All rights reserved.

Copyright © 2004 by Osprey Publishing Limited

Library of Congress Catalog Card Number: 2004050382
ISBN: 0-275-98447-8
ISSN: 1547-206X

Praeger Publishers, 88 Post Road West, Westport, CT 06881
An imprint of Greenwood Publishing Group, Inc.
www.praeger.com

Printed in China through World Print Ltd.

The paper used in this book complies with the Permanent Paper Standard issued
by the National Information Standards Organization (Z39.48-1984).

10 9 8 7 6 5 4 3 2 1

ILLUSTRATED BY: Mike Adams

CONTENTS

KEY TO MILITARY SYMBOLS

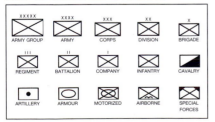

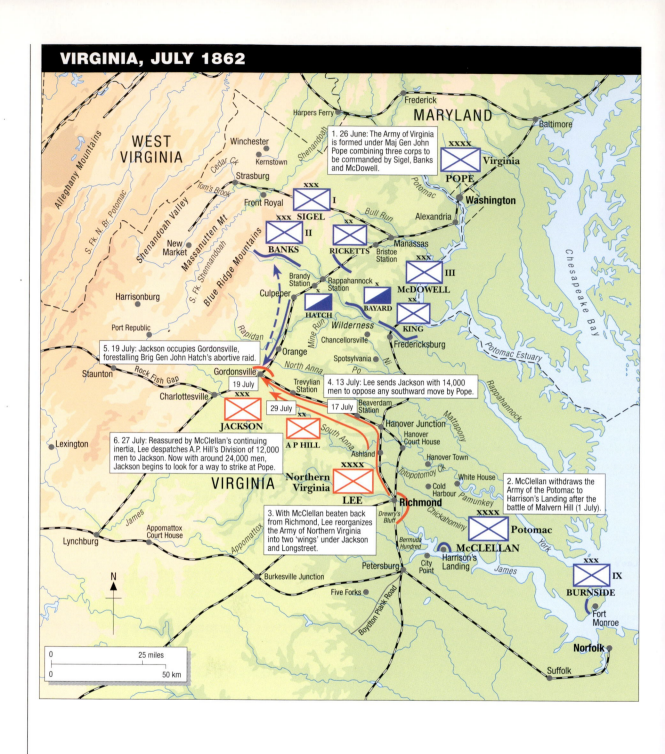

VIRGINIA, JULY 1862

1. 26 June: The Army of Virginia is formed under Maj Gen John Pope combining three corps to be commanded by Sigel, Banks and McDowell.

5. 19 July: Jackson occupies Gordonsville, forestalling Brig Gen John Hatch's abortive raid.

4. 13 July: Lee sends Jackson with 14,000 men to oppose any southward move by Pope.

6. 27 July: Reassured by McClellan's continuing inertia, Lee despatches A.P. Hill's Division of 12,000 men to Jackson. Now with around 24,000 men, Jackson begins to look for a way to strike at Pope.

2. McClellan withdraws the Army of the Potomac to Harrison's Landing after the battle of Malvern Hill (1 July).

3. With McClellan beaten back from Richmond, Lee reorganizes the Army of Northern Virginia into two 'wings' under Jackson and Longstreet.

ORIGINS OF THE CAMPAIGN

Reserved Virginian Robert E. Lee's masterful handling of operations, during the Second Manassas campaign, did much to establish him as the premier military leader of the Confederate States of America. NA

From the fall of Fort Sumter in South Carolina on 14 April 1861, the first year of the Civil War had gone badly for the Union. The first major engagement between the two untested armies demonstrated the Federals' typical poor showing during the course of the early fighting. On 21 July, Major General Irvin McDowell's Yankees fled from the Confederates under the overall command of General Joseph E. Johnston at the Battle of Bull Run, as the North called it, or the Battle of Manassas, as the Southern victors referred to the brief encounter.

After this débâcle President Abraham Lincoln immediately set out to find a military man who would not fail him as McDowell had. He also sought a winning strategy to crush the Rebels. "Old Abe" quickly settled upon one key strategic goal – the capture of the capital of the Confederate States of America at Richmond, Virginia. And the man who Lincoln thought could achieve this was a self-styled "Napoleon of the New World," Major General George B. McClellan. During late July 1861 the diminutive major general had been responsible for establishing Washington, DC's defenses. This was much to Lincoln's relief because he was apprehensive about his own capital becoming the target of the Confederate forces.

With this accomplishment to his credit, Northern officials tasked "Little Mac" with the creation of what would become the Army of the Potomac. Once he had forged the Federal soldiers into this mighty weapon McClellan proposed to move by sea and assemble at Fort Monroe, Virginia. This Federal bastion was about seven days' march from Richmond, and thus a logical staging area for McClellan's proposed invasion.

By March 1862 McClellan had assembled a sufficiently powerful force to begin his move to the Virginia Peninsula. He had hoped for more troops, but Lincoln, fearing for Washington's security, refused McDowell, who was by now relegated to the command of a corps, permission to send his 40,000 soldiers with McClellan. Instead McDowell's I Corps was retained in the vicinity of Manassas where the defeat of the previous year doubtless remained fresh in his mind.

This was only one of the problems that plagued McClellan's bid to capture Richmond. Indeed, his own inability to take decisive action resulted in a month's delay in the unnecessary siege of Yorktown. That costly decision allowed Confederate General Johnston to bring up his army to face McClellan. McClellan had ordered siege artillery to be brought up from Washington, but two days before his bombardment was due to begin Johnston withdrew toward Richmond. McClellan pursued the retreating Johnston slowly to within a few miles of the seat of the Confederate government. McClellan still hoped that McDowell, by now at Fredericksburg, would join him and further bolster his numbers. This would only be possible if another Union command under General Nathaniel Banks, could secure northern Virginia's strategic Shenandoah Valley. The valley was both a valuable source of food and materials for the Confederacy and a possible route for a Southern attack on Washington. McDowell's forces at Fredericksburg would not be released to McClellan until any potential threat from the Shenandoah Valley had been dealt with.

General Thomas "Stonewall" Jackson's lightning Shenandoah Valley campaign in May and June 1862 showed the threat was far from dealt with. With 18,000 men, Jackson ran rings around numerous separate Union commands that in total outnumbered him almost four-to-one. In the spring, Jackson rode roughshod over not only Banks's men but also those of McDowell and a third command under the original standard bearer of the Republican party, John Charles Frémont. Attacking the fragmented Union corps in the Valley, Jackson won a series of victories at McDowell (8 May), Front Royal (23 May), Winchester (25 May), Cross Keys (8 June) and Port Republic (9 June).

Such was the effect of the victories won by Stonewall Jackson and his "foot cavalry", an honorific bestowed on Jackson's men as a result of their lightning movement and aggressive tactics during the Valley campaign, that they were able to rejoin the Army of Northern Virginia to assist in the defense of Richmond. With General Johnston having been wounded at Seven Pines (Fair Oaks), General Robert E. Lee had now taken command.

It became clear to Lincoln that he had to address a number of issues as the summer of 1862 brought further bad news to the Northern cause. After the intensive Seven Days campaign, in which McClellan failed to overwhelm the Confederate defenders of Richmond, Lincoln considered new candidates for the post of general-in-chief. A well respected West Point graduate, Henry Halleck, was seen as the heir apparent, but he would be cast more as a chief of staff than a field leader.

Furthermore, the president realized the disjointed commands that Jackson had humiliated needed to be consolidated under one man. This individual might also be a potential replacement for McClellan as the field commander of the Union Army. As such, it was necessary to find a contender with the right qualities, not the least of which was actual victory against a major Southern force. There was no one who could make that claim in the eastern theater, but fighting in the western theater had been less one sided. There, some Northerners had demonstrated grit and the ability to win. The western theater seemed to Lincoln the most fertile ground to seek a fighting general during that bleak summer of 1862.

Union survivors built an obelisk near the Brawner farmhouse to commemorate the deadly contest at Second Bull Run, the Northern name for this engagement. The opposing sides often gave different titles to battles.

CHRONOLOGY

1861

12 April – General P.G.T. Beauregard orders the attack on Fort Sumter,

15 April – Union President Abraham Lincoln calls upon the loyal states to furnish 75,000 volunteers.

21 July – First Battle of Bull Run (Manassas) Irwin McDowell suffers the Union's first major defeat in the field.

1862

28 February–8 April – Relative inactivity in the eastern theater of operations contrasts with fighting further west along the Mississippi River where the Battle of New Madrid and the fall of Island No.10 brings recognition to Union Major General John Pope.

April–May – Peninsula Campaign planned and led by Lincoln's new choice for a Union commander, 35-year-old George B. McClellan. The move to encircle Richmond's defenses does not succeed.

23 March–9 June – In an effort to weaken the Union field force and thereby decrease the threat to Richmond, Confederate authorities dispatch Thomas "Stonewall" Jackson to the Shenandoah Valley, thereby drawing away the equivalent of three Federal divisions. Jackson succeeds in neutralizing or defeating a series of separate Northern commands and also prevents McDowell from sending reinforcements to McClellan.

31 May–1 June – Battle of Seven Pines (Fair Oaks) Confederate General Joseph E. Johnston sustains a severe wound prompting Confederate President Jefferson Davis to replace the stricken commander with Robert E. Lee.

26 June – President Lincoln appoints Major General John Pope as the commander of the newly created Army of Virginia, unifying the previously three separate corps commanded by Generals Banks, McDowell, and Sigel.

26 June–2 July – Seven Days' Battles are waged as Robert E. Lee's Army of Northern Virginia pushes McClellan's Army of the Potomac back from the gates of Richmond.

11 July – Searching for a commander who can bring victory to the North, Lincoln names Major General Henry Halleck as Union General-in-Chief.

9 August – The second Manassas campaign opens with its first major engagement at Battle of Cedar Mountain (Cedar Run/Slaughter Mountain), fought as Jackson's Wing attempts to cripple an isolated portion of Pope's Army of Virginia

22 August – "Jeb" Stuart's raid on Catlett Station fails to destroy the Cedar Run railroad bridge, which will not burn because rain has soaked its timbers, but he captures General Pope's dispatch book, providing General Lee with information on Union troop dispositions.

23 August – Clashes at Beverly's, Freeman's, and Kelly's Fords as the Confederates test Pope's defenses along the Rappahannock River.

3.00am, 25 August – Jackson's Wing marches for Sulphur Springs to begin a wide flanking movement around the Union right flank. That night it camps near Salem.

26 August – Jackson's men capture Bristoe Station and the huge Federal depot at Manassas Junction.

Confederate General Thomas "Stonewall" Jackson would lead his men with distinction at Manassas (the Southern name for the two battles known in the North as Bull Run) both in 1861, and again in 1862. Religious fervor was among his many traits. Here some of his loyal men join their colorful commander in prayer. NA

27 August – As Union forces attempt to trap him, Jackson withdraws from Manassas in three columns. He redeploys his men north-west of Groveton.

28 August – With Pope having failed to locate his forces, Jackson's Wing emerges to attack King's Federal Division on the march at Brawner's Farm (Groveton). Brigadier General John Gibbon's Brigade bears the brunt of the fighting. Late in the afternoon Longstreet's Wing captures Thoroughfare Gap in the Bull Run Mountains. The route to Manassas is now clear.

29 August – General Pope opens the battle of Second Manassas with a series of piecemeal attacks against Jackson's troops, who are defending the line of an unfinished railroad north of Groveton. The Confederates repulse the disjointed attacks.

30 August – Unknown to Pope, Longstreet has joined Jackson and launches an attack against the Federal left flank, while Pope continues to hammer Jackson's line. Eventually the Federals are flanked. Determined rearguard fighting as Pope's men withdraw saves his army from annihilation.

31 August – skirmish at Germantown as Pope reorganizes his chaotic army at Centreville. Jackson's Wing begins a flank march to Fairfax.

1 September – Battle of Chantilly (Ox Hill) as Stevens' and Kearny's divisions block Jackson's flank march. Both Stevens and Kearny are killed.

4 September – The Army of Northern Virginia crosses the Potomac on march to Maryland.

12–15 September – Harper's Ferry, Virginia, under attack by Jackson.

17–18 September – Lee's Army of Northern Virginia and McClellan's Army of the Potomac clash at the Battle of Antietam (Sharpsburg) in the bloodiest single day of the war.

22 September – Lincoln issues the Emancipation Proclamation.

OPPOSING COMMANDERS

UNION

John Pope

When Lincoln reached the conclusion that McClellan was not the man to bring the war to an end, he turned to a fellow native of Kentucky – John Pope. Pope, like Lincoln, had left this state and relocated to Illinois, and it was from here that he received an appointment to the United States Military Academy. After graduation in 1842, his class standing (17 out of 56) was high enough to secure a posting to the prestigious Corps of Topographical Engineers.

Pope eventually ended up apparently trapped in the backwater of Maine, but he was rescued by the outbreak of the Mexican War in 1846. His service and valor in this conflict earned him promotion to brevet captain.

By 1 July 1856 Pope had advanced to a captaincy in the Topographical Engineers, a rank he held until 14 June 1861. On that day, having had the good fortune to serve as an escort officer accompanying Lincoln to the inauguration, and because of other ties to the new chief executive, he was advanced to a brigadier of volunteers. During the next year he held various commands in Missouri, serving under John C. Frémont. His performance was such that he ultimately was put in charge of operations along the Mississippi River.

By early 1862, after victories at New Madrid and the Mississippi River's Island No. 10, he was made commander of one of the three field

During July 1861, at the Battle of First Manassas, Jackson made "Portici" his headquarters. Over 12 months later, the din of muskets and cannon could again be heard in the vicinity of this stately home. LC

armies led by Henry W. Halleck toward Corinth, Mississippi. He soon added a second star to his shoulder straps when he was appointed a major general of US Volunteers on 21 March 1862. All this put him in line for consideration when Lincoln decided to combine the three divided Union commands in northern Virginia, which had all failed to bring Jackson to bay in the Shenandoah Valley.

With the disparate corps combined into the Army of Virginia, Pope took charge of the organization on 26 June 1862. Frémont would not serve under his former subordinate, and was replaced by another officer. He was not the only one to disdain Pope, who became unpopular with many of his fellow officers, as well as the rank and file. This bad feeling could be traced to the early days of Pope's command of the Army of Virginia. He issued a pompous communiqué to his new command boasting: "Let us understand each other. I have come to you from the West, where we have always seen the backs of our enemies; whose business it has been to seek the adversary, and to best him where he was found; whose policy had been attack and not defense." Not only did these words grate with McClellan and his supporters, but they also raised the hackles of the troops in the Army of Virginia, many of whom had been serving in the theater for some time and resented being portrayed as ineffective or even worse, cowardly!

In another unfortunate piece of bombast, Pope claimed his headquarters would be in the saddle. This boast backfired with several of Pope's peers maintaining he had his "headquarters where his hindquarters" ought to be.

Lincoln unilaterally selected Pope as a "western man" who could prosecute the war, but his choice of champion did more than antagonize the forces of the eastern theater, however. Pope became a target for particular hatred in the South by prescribing harsh treatment of Confederate sympathizers. Virginians in areas controlled by his troops were to be brought in and instructed to take the oath of allegiance to the United States. If they balked, they were to be turned out from their homes and expelled to enemy territory. Additionally, not only did he order his troops to live off the land, but also directed that guerrillas were to be executed as traitors when captured. Furthermore,

TOP **Major General George B. McClellan (center) had been hailed as the man who would bring swift victory for the North. "Little Mac" did not live up to expectations, although he continued to command the Army of the Potomac after he failed to capture Richmond. Many other generals in this group portrait would serve at the Battle of Second Bull Run. NA**

ABOVE **Known as "Old Brains" Major General Henry Wagner Halleck assumed duties as general-in-chief of the Union Army during the summer of 1862. He was a good administrator, but lacked strategic capabilities and the strong leadership needed to direct his fellow Union generals during the campaign that brought the Northern and Southern armies back to Bull Run. NA**

five local civilians of prominence were to be rounded up and put to death if partisans shot at his men.

In this foretaste of the total war concept practised so effectively later by Ulysses Grant, Pope provoked the usually mild-mannered Lee in a way that no other adversary ever had. Lee developed a personal enmity toward Pope, referring to him as a "miscreant" who had to be "suppressed."

In response, the Confederate government made it known that Pope and his officers would not be accorded consideration as soldiers. If caught they would be held prisoner so long as Pope's odious dictates remained in effect. Should Southern civilians be killed, a like number of Federal prisoners would be sent to the gallows.

These harsh measures were not carried out and after the Second Manassas campaign the point became moot. In fact, at that time Lincoln also lost faith in his protégé and shortly after Pope's defeat in northern Virginia he was transferred.

For most of the remainder of the war Pope oversaw the Department of the Northwest, and among other things dealt with the 1864 Sioux uprising in Minnesota. Having redeemed himself in the eyes of the administration, in 1865 he received a brevet as a regular army major general in recognition of his actions at Island No.10. The following year he mustered out of the volunteers, but returned to the regulars where he served as departmental commander in various locations until his retirement in 1886. Six years later he died.

Henry Halleck

At the same time that Lincoln was looking for an alternative to McClellan as his eastern field commander, he was also seeking to replace McClellan as general-in-chief. On 11 July 1862 Henry Halleck, a New York native and Military Academy graduate (1839), was given the mantel previously worn by Winfield Scott and George McClellan.

An engineer officer who had been breveted for his performance in Mexico, Halleck previously had overseen construction of coastal

Disappointed with McClellan's performance, President Abraham Lincoln cast about for a new head for his army. He now pinned his hopes on John Pope, who despite much bravado was no match for the opposition he encountered at Second Bull Run. Pope's shortcomings proved costly, opening the way for the Confederates to bring the war north. NA

Major General Irvin McDowell had commanded at First Bull Run, but his reputation suffered greatly as the Union Army left the field in disarray. During the summer of 1862 McDowell, seen here (center) with his staff, was to return to the scene of this earlier Federal defeat. NA

In 1852 Franz Sigel journeyed from his native Baden in Germany to the United States. He was outspoken and held liberal views, leading him to support the unsuccessful Revolution of 1848 against Prussia. The former army officer fled his native land, which brought him to St. Louis, Missouri. His influence among the German community led to him being commissioned as a brigadier general of volunteers soon after the Civil War began. NA

fortifications, served as a member of the faculty at West Point, and conducted a study of France's military. These endeavors and his writings *Report on the Means of National Defense* and *Elements of Military Art and Science*, along with a translation of the influential French volume *Vie Politique et Militaire de Napoleon* by Henri Jomini, earned him the nickname of "Old Brains" but this sobriquet became derogatory during the Civil War.

Although Halleck had left the army in 1854 to establish a law practice in California, he continued his interest in the profession of arms. When the war broke out, Winfield Scott recommended Halleck be given an important assignment, and as such, on 19 August 1861, he was commissioned a major general in the US Army.

After modest accomplishments in the western theater of operations he was called to Washington, where it was believed his administrative capabilities would bear fruit in galvanizing the Union army into a viable force. This was not to prove the case, however, and a number of his subordinates criticized him for a failure to clearly communicate both what was expected of them and the actions of the various commands. To some degree both of these characteristics were evident during the Second Manassas campaign.

Furthermore, Halleck tended to attribute failures to others, thereby alienating most of his fellow generals. Consequently, he was finally reassigned as the army's chief of staff, and in this role performed well, although he remained one of the most unpopular men in Washington.

At war's end he remained in uniform, first as commander in Virginia and later as head of the Military Division of the Pacific. In 1872 he died while serving in Louisville, Kentucky.

Nathaniel Banks

Massachusetts governor "Bobbin Boy" Banks, who had been speaker of the state's lower house, and for a time one of its US congressmen, was just one of many political appointees to be named a general in the Union volunteers. With no military background, he remained in divisional and departmental commands near the capital during the early stages of the war, but was then sent to the Shenandoah Valley. The Confederates under Stonewall Jackson outfought the politician-turned-

Massachusetts governor Nathaniel P. "Bobbin Boy" Banks was just one of many political appointees to be named a general in the Union volunteers. Lacking a military background, he remained in divisional and departmental commands near the capital during the early stages of the war, but by the time of Second Manassas was II Corps commander in the Army of Virginia.

soldier, and after capturing a significant cache of his supplies jokingly referred to him as "Commissary Banks".

Not long after Banks was assigned to the Army of Virginia, Jackson goaded him again at Cedar Mountain, then once more faced him at Second Manassas. After a short assignment in Washington, the administration shipped him to New Orleans as Benjamin F. "Beast" Butler's replacement. In that command Port Hudson was his first target, but he failed to overcome the defenses until after Vicksburg had been taken by Grant.

His effectiveness during the Red River Campaign of 1864 was little better. Despite such lackluster martial performances, Congress decided to honor him with a resolution of thanks. Banks mustered out of the volunteers on 24 August 1865 and returned to politics.

Irvin McDowell

As a young man Irvin McDowell attended the Collège de Troyes in France, then went on to the US Military Academy where he graduated 23rd of 45 cadets in his class of 1838. He was commissioned in the artillery, with a stint of frontier duty before returning to West Point as a tactics instructor and adjutant.

During the Mexican War he became General John Wool's aide de camp and adjutant, followed by another posting to the frontier. He ultimately secured a transfer to army headquarters in Washington. While serving there, Winfield Scott introduced him to a number of influential members of Lincoln's administration. Secretary of the Treasury Samuel Chase particularly championed his cause and was instrumental in obtaining Major McDowell a promotion to brigadier general in the Regular Army on 14 May 1861. Two weeks later he assumed command of forces south of the Potomac and in the vicinity of the capital.

McDowell was not to remain encamped for long, however. Political pressures and the short term of enlistment of some of his troops, forced him to lead his unprepared army to Manassas. Part of his command marched against Blackburn's Ford along Bull Run. A few days later McDowell launched his main attack, which resulted in the First Battle of Manassas (Bull Run). The failure of Union arms at First Manassas brought an end to his rapid rise. Four days after this defeat, McClellan assumed control, while on 3 October McDowell was assigned a division. After the Army of the Potomac was organized, he gained a better berth, being entrusted with I Corps. His first assignment was the protection of Washington as McClellan began the Peninsula Campaign. In due course his men were to proceed overland to support McClellan in his drive against Richmond, but as events transpired McDowell and his men were diverted to face Jackson in the Shenandoah Valley.

Following this unsuccessful effort, he was assigned III Corps in Pope's Army of Virginia. In that capacity he participated in the actions at Cedar Mountain and Rappahannock Station. Several years later the former engagement gained him a major-general's brevet in the Regular Army.

In the wake of Second Manassas he was relieved from his command, being singled out as one of the parties responsible for the Union defeat. He requested a court of inquiry, and was absolved of blame for the débâcle; a fate not shared by fellow Union general Fitz John Porter, who became the scapegoat for the loss, not clearing his name until many years after the war.

South Carolinian James Longstreet began his military career as a cadet at West Point, graduating in 1842. Commissioned as a second lieutenant in the infantry, he served in the Mexican War where he was wounded at Chapultepec. He subsequently became a major in the US Army Paymaster Department. On 1 June 1861, Longstreet, who would come to be known variously as "Old Pete" and "Old War Horse", resigned his commission to join the Confederate forces. Longstreet's performance in various engagements during the early stages of the war gained him Lee's confidence, as a result of which he was given command of a "wing" of the Army of Northern Virginia. NA

Although McDowell managed to lift this cloud from his record, he would not receive another field command. Instead he served on commissions and boards in Washington until 1 July 1864 when he was sent west to take over the Department of the Pacific, which was then headquartered in San Francisco.

On 1 September 1866, McDowell mustered out of volunteer service, but secured a billet as a brigadier general in the Regular Army, and six years later advanced to major general, the grade at which he retired in 1882. He ultimately became park commissioner for the City of San Francisco.

Franz Sigel

In 1852 Franz Sigel left his native Baden bound for the United States. He was an outspoken liberal, and had supported the unsuccessful Revolution of 1848 against Prussia. This former army officer was subsequently forced to flee his native land, and not long after landing in his new country, he made his way to St. Louis, Missouri. He worked there for nearly a decade as a schoolteacher. Then, in 1861, having become something of a pillar of the influential German population in the area, he attracted Lincoln's attention. The president desired to win support among transplanted Europeans with an anti-slavery, Unionist bent. With this objective in mind, during the summer of 1861, Sigel was commissioned as a brigadier general of volunteers.

Thereafter he became active in Missouri, fighting at the Battle of Wilson's Creek. On 8 March 1862, he commanded two divisions at the Battle of Pea Ridge, helping defeat Southern troops under Major General Earl Van Dorn.

Promotion to major general followed on 22 March 1862. Soon afterwards he was brought to the eastern theater to face Jackson in the Shenandoah Valley. When Pope was selected to command the Army of Virginia, Sigel was appointed commander of I Corps. Following the Second Manassas campaign he briefly commanded XI Corps in the Army of the Potomac, but his military career was lackluster at best after that. Sigel's defeat at the Battle of New Market (15 May 1864), led to his removal from field command. Almost a year later he resigned his commission, returning to civilian pursuits until his death in 1902.

CONFEDERATE

Robert E. Lee

As the son of a Revolutionary War hero it came as no surprise when young Robert E. Lee obtained an appointment to West Point. He entered the academy in 1825, and after four years as a cadet had managed to avoid receiving even one demerit. In addition, he graduated second in his class of 1829, which earned him a commission as second lieutenant in the Corps of Engineers.

His first assignment to work on fortifications at Hampton Roads was followed by a detail to serve as an assistant to the chief of engineers, a duty that began in 1834. This posting to Washington allowed him to live in a fine home that his new bride's family had given the couple. The stately home still stands overlooking Arlington National Cemetery.

Lee then went on to other duties, not the least of which was on Winfield Scott's staff during the Mexican War, where he served at both Cerro Gordo and Churubusco. He conducted reconnaissance during this period that greatly assisted the movement of Scott's forces. His services brought three brevets and Scott's highest accolade. He ultimately pronounced Lee "the very best soldier that I ever saw in the field."

Lee went on to become the commanding officer of the 2nd US Cavalry, and later the superintendent of West Point. Soon after the Civil War began, Lee's first-class reputation prompted Lincoln to offer him command of the Federal Army. He declined then resigned his commission, offering his services to his native state of Virginia.

On 23 April 1861, his offer was accepted with the rank of major general in the Virginia state forces. By 14 May he was also commissioned as brigadier general in the Confederate Regular Army. A month later he jumped to full general.

Jefferson Davis quickly appointed him as his military advisor, but after Joseph Johnston was wounded at Seven Pines, Lee departed Richmond to replace him. Thereafter, he remained in the field for the duration of the war, gaining many laurels and a legendary status. President Jefferson Davis ultimately appointed him general in chief of the Confederate States Army on 31 January 1865. It was, however, far too late for even Lee's prodigious talents to turn the tide.

Lee was a very different type of military leader from Pope, except in one respect. He, too, sought a classic confrontation in the mold of Austerlitz. According to eminent military historian Russell Weigley, at Second Manassas Lee "came as close as any general since Napoleon to duplicating the Napoleonic system of battlefield victory by fixing the enemy in a position with a detachment, bringing the rest of the army onto his flank and rear, and then routing him from the flank." It was a perfect textbook execution, but as Weigley concluded: "Lee was too Napoleonic. Like Napoleon himself, with his passion for the strategy of annihilation and the climactic decisive battle as its expression, he destroyed in the end not the enemy armies, but his own."

James Longstreet

South Carolinian James Longstreet began his military career as a cadet at West Point, graduating in 1842, as one of John Pope's classmates. He then received his commission as a second lieutenant in the infantry, and his first field duty was in Florida. After that he served in the Mexican War where he received a wound at Chapultepec. His actions in this conflict brought two brevets. Duty on the frontier followed, but eventually he transferred to the Paymaster Department and there he secured the rank of major.

On 1 June 1861, he resigned his US Army commission and sought a post as paymaster with the Confederate forces. Instead, on 17 June, he was made a brigadier general and placed in command of a brigade. By early October, he rose to the rank of major general, at which time he became a divisional commander. He subsequently participated in the Peninsula Campaign, Yorktown, Williamsburg, Seven Pines, and the Seven Days.

His performance in these various engagements gained Lee's confidence. Because of this he was placed in charge of a "wing" of Lee's

Except for Robert E. Lee, no other Confederate commander gained such renown or was more exalted than Thomas J. Jackson. A graduate of the class of 1846 at West Point, Jackson had served in the artillery in the Mexican War, where he earned two brevets. After the war he resigned his commission, and took up a post at the Virginia Military Institute, where the humorless professor no doubt would have remained in obscurity had it not been for the Civil War. Certainly an eccentric he was undoubtedly one of the South's boldest and most aggressive commanders. He played a key role in the Confederate prosecution of the war until his tragic death following the battle of Chancellorsville. NA

forces, a term that was pressed into service at that time to evade a piece of early Confederate legislation that disallowed organizations larger than a division. Ultimately Lee was able to have this prohibition repealed, and at that point Longstreet officially took command of I Corps of the Army of Northern Virginia, which in addition to other elements contained over 50 per cent of that army's infantry.

Although he was not as aggressive in pressing the enemy at Second Manassas as Lee may have wished, Longstreet nevertheless generally served his superior well. In fact, Longstreet's seizing of Thoroughfare Gap proved pivotal in the ultimate routing of Pope's troops. This accomplishment and his actions at Sharpsburg soon thereafter, led to his promotion to the rank of lieutenant general.

His friends sometimes called him "Pete" but to others he became Lee's "Old War Horse". Despite this latter title, his inclination toward strategic offense and tactical defense differed from that of his superior. While Longstreet's philosophy was correct in some instances, such as at Gettysburg, his incapacity for independent operations marred his reputation. Whatever Longstreet's shortcomings, he remained at Lee's side until the final surrender at Appomattox.

Thomas J. Jackson

Except for Robert E. Lee, no other Confederate commander gained such renown or was more exalted than Thomas J. Jackson. A graduate of the class of 1846 at West Point, Jackson had served in the artillery in the Mexican War, where he earned two brevets. After the war he resigned his commission then took up a post at the Virginia Military Institute, where the humorless professor no doubt would have remained in obscurity had it not been for the Civil War. Cadets considered him peculiar to

At the outbreak of the war some Union troops appeared in gray uniforms, as shown in this portrait of Henry H. Richardson, a subaltern with Company F of the 21st Massachusetts Volunteer Infantry. This regiment fought at Henry Hill on 30 August 1862. USAMHI

Some of Irvin McDowell's men encamped at Culpeper, Virginia, a town that boasted a key depot on the Orange & Alexandria Railroad. The seated man appears in the typical combat uniform that came to be associated with the Union Army – the dark blue "bummer's" cap, with dark blue, four-button sack coat and sky-blue kersey trousers. USAMHI

say the least, and they gave him such nicknames as "Tom Fool Jackson" and "Old Blue Light", in the latter instance because of his penetrating blue eyes.

When war came he accepted a colonelcy in the Virginia forces. He was soon ordered to the Union arsenal at Harpers Ferry. From there he marched with Joseph Johnston, as commander of 1st Brigade, Army of the Shenandoah. Newly promoted to brigadier general on 17 June 1861, Jackson was part of Johnston's army that moved to unite with Brigadier General Pierre Beauregard's troops at Manassas. Jackson's conduct during the subsequent First Battle of Manassas gained both he and his brigade the name "Stonewall".

By the fall he was a major general with responsibility for the strategically important Shenandoah Valley. He would again sting the enemy, but not always with the desired results. For instance, at Kernstown (23 March 1862) he suffered a defeat, for which the pious soldier partially blamed himself because he had fought on a Sunday. Nevertheless, he was able to divert Federal reinforcements to the valley and away from the attack on Richmond.

In May Jackson's performance improved. He halted Major General John C. Frémont's advance from West Virginia at McDowell, then took the offensive against a number of other Union commanders, none of whom could bring him to bay. His victories in the Valley Campaign behind him, Lee ordered Stonewall to assist in the defense of Richmond.

Once George McClellan had withdrawn after the Seven Days battles, Lee sent Jackson north, informing him in a letter, "I want Pope to be suppressed … " Knowing Jackson's propensity to keep his plans to himself, Lee's missive also suggested, "advising with your division commanders as to your movements, much trouble will be saved you in arranging details, and they can act more intelligently." Unfortunately, Jackson never took this sage counsel to heart.

At Cedar Mountain he committed his forces piecemeal, suffering unnecessary casualties in his eagerness to engage General Banks's Corps. His flanking movement later in the Manassas campaign was executed with great daring and threw Pope's Army of Virginia off balance. He then held firm in the face of determined attacks until Longstreet was able to roll up the Union left flank.

After Second Manassas, Lee once again detached Jackson and charged him with the seizure of Harpers Ferry. He subsequently rejoined Lee at Sharpsburg. Then came another promotion and command of II Corps.

Fredericksburg followed; then Chancellorsville, where his men outflanked the Union right and devastated the XI Corps of the Army of the Potomac. Later that night, as Jackson was returning from a reconnaissance, some of his own men opened fire, striking him in the arm which was amputated. Complications set in, and on 10 May 1863 he died of pneumonia, depriving the South of one of her greatest commanders.

Matthew Brady captured another gray uniform worn by a Northern officer, in this case an ornate example donned by the one-time commander of the 5th New York, Abram Duryée. Early in the war Duryée put aside this outfit for a brigadier general's uniform. At Second Manassas he commanded the 1st Brigade, 2nd Division of III Corps, under McDowell. During the battle he received two wounds, but nevertheless continued on active duty. USAMHI

OPPOSING PLANS

Lee's Strategic Envelopment

Despite McClellan's failure to capture Richmond, his powerful army remained a threat that concerned Lee and the Confederate leadership in general. It was vital that any steps taken to engage the enemy elsewhere did not jeopardize the Confederate capital. To accomplish the twin objectives of moving the fighting away from Richmond without endangering the city, Lee conceived a bold plan.

Although the enemy's 75,000 men outnumbered his 55,000, Lee decided to split his forces. One half of his army was to undertake a wide strategic envelopment with the purpose of flanking the Union line of communications and forcing the enemy to do battle at a place and time of Lee's choosing. This move would draw away forces from McClellan or at least divert other units from reinforcing him, especially if there was any hint that Washington, DC, might be threatened in the process.

Lee's scheme relied on swiftness and eluding the enemy. All the skill his subordinates could muster would be required to make the daring plan work. If he failed, however, the effect might be the opposite of that desired. The possibility existed that much of his force, if not all of it, could fall prey to the superior numbers of the Federal Army. If Lee accomplished his objective he would stand between the enemy and Washington, a position that would put the Federal Army on the

The 2nd US Sharpshooters were decked out in green uniforms, a shade long associated with riflemen. Lieutenant R.B. Calef was one of the officers in this special organization, which carried the breech-loading Sharps rifle, by the time it underwent its baptism of fire at Second Manassas. USAMHI

Weighing in at less than 100 lbs, Confederate Brigadier General William "Scrappy Billy" Mahone commanded a brigade in one of Longstreet's divisions. His pleated blouse and light-colored campaign hat offer just one example of the many variations of uniform worn by Southern officers and enlisted men alike. Note the wreath around his three stars on his collar, the common designation for most general officers in the Confederate forces. USAMHI

defensive, and in turn keep them away from Richmond. Of equal importance, a decisive victory against the North might encourage recognition of the Confederacy by European powers.

With stakes this high, Lee was willing to gamble, yet he could not afford to be reckless. Because McClellan was but 20 miles from Richmond at Harrison's Landing, and Pope's new Army of Virginia within striking distance, Lee was not in a position to take to the field himself. In fact, if Pope decided to mobilize and march on Richmond, the consequences could be disastrous. As such, not until early August, when Lee learned that McClellan was withdrawing on transports to head down river, did he have the latitude to move his immediate command for a thrust against Pope.

Pope's Mission

Jackson's success against the dispersed Union corps during the Shenandoah Campaign had resulted in the decision to create a unified command structure to better utilize the Northern forces in that area. Once Pope was in place Lincoln had two strong armies at his disposal, but the question was how best to deploy them. On taking command of the Army of Virginia, Pope was given three main priorities. He would not allow the capital to be threatened; he had to protect the Shenandoah Valley; and he should use his forces to pose a threat to the Confederates and attempt to draw Lee away from the defense of Richmond.

Pope loudly proclaimed to Lincoln and anyone else who would listen, that he was the right man for this task. If McClellan's army was added to his, Pope also felt that he would be in a position to engage in a Napoleonic-style clash that would crush the Army of Northern Virginia, leaving the road to Richmond open for his conquest. This is what the administration and many other Northerners wanted to hear.

Lincoln, in particular, paid attention to Pope's words. He and certain Northern leaders believed that harsher measures were required to quell the rebellion. To this end, the President intended to use the Confiscation Act passed by the US Senate in July 1862. This law authorized the seizure of Confederate property for the promulgation of the war, including the confiscation of slaves; a power that Lincoln hoped to exercise soon. With this end in mind he drafted an Emancipation Proclamation that would deprive the South of a major resource, namely slaves. At the same time it would send a clear message to England and other important European powers that the Confederacy was fighting for an unjust cause, which should not justifiably be supported by foreign nations.

Thus Pope received significant political support for his aggressive stance. Lincoln hoped for a major victory that would allow him to proclaim emancipation. If Pope gave him that victory he would become a national hero, and no doubt be rewarded with leadership of the Union forces.

Certainly Pope shared Lincoln's predilection to deal sternly with the South in so far as prosecution of the war was concerned. He made it clear that guerrilla activities within his area would be dealt with severely. Additionally, Pope intended to live off the land, destroy vital Confederate transportation assets, and if possible cut Lee off from Jackson. In order to accomplish all this he had to act swiftly to consolidate his forces. Although more aggressive than McClellan, who tended to have the "slows", Pope's bellicose manner would not prove any more successful.

OPPOSING ARMIES

UNION TROOPS

After the opening salvos at Fort Sumter, war fever gripped the North. At first recruiting proved easy. Thousands of men responded to President Lincoln's 15 April call for 75,000 volunteers to sign on for three months' service. Each state received a quota, and there was little difficulty in supplying the numbers required. Many flocked to the colors in part because they believed the war would be short. Indeed, a number of units had been raised for only a half-year's service.

By the summer of 1862, however, a goodly number of the original six month volunteers had returned home. They were replaced by some 640,000 volunteers who had entered the Northern ranks thereafter, usually with long enlistment periods. State troops and volunteers dominated, as indicated by the fact that Regular Army personnel totaled only 23,308 artillery, cavalry, infantry, and support troops by 31 March 1862, as opposed to 613,818 volunteers and a substantial number of militiamen. These

Some Regular Army and volunteer units alike continued to wear the long nine-button frock coat and black hat looped up on the side that had been regulation prior to the war. Men of the 2nd Wisconsin Infantry were among this group. As a consequence, they and their comrades in the 6th and 7th Wisconsin, along with the 19th Indiana, came to be called the "Black Hat Brigade". They likewise were referred to as the "Iron Brigade", a nickname they earned after stalwart performances at both Second Manassas and Antietam. NA

would be the men who carried the Union banner at Second Manassas, most of whom were infantrymen clad in a variety of uniform styles and colors and carrying an array of small arms or manning numerous types of field pieces in the case of the artillerymen assigned to Pope's command.

Most of the Yankees had not seen action before. For instance, the 2nd US Sharpshooters under Colonel Henry A. Post, who had been assigned to Irvin McDowell's Corps during the Peninsula Campaign, never made it into battle during George McClellan's bid to take Richmond. Thus the specially armed regiment with its Sharps rifles had not been able to employ their breech loaders and marksmanship skills against the enemy. This situation would change soon.

The green-clad Sharpshooter regiment was formed into eight companies rather than the typical ten. Furthermore, most other regiments were made up of men from one state, but not so with these Sharpshooters. Company A had been raised from Minnesota, B from Michigan, C from Pennsylvania, D from Maine, E and H from Vermont, and F and G from New Hampshire.

The 5th New York (or Duryée's Zouaves as they were known in honor of their colonel, Abram Duryée) were more typical, in that the regiment consisted of ten companies raised from one area; New York. Duryée had seen to it that his men were attired in red fezzes and baggy trousers of a matching shade, along with white gaiters and jaunty blue jackets that reached just above the waist. Their flamboyant uniforms were based on those worn by France's famed colonial troops. Although they may have looked like dandies to the uninitiated, these colorful infantrymen from New York had seen service during the Peninsula Campaign and were considered to be excellent troops. Like many of the units who had been in that campaign as part of the Army of the Potomac, they were intensely loyal to McClellan, and not particularly pleased to have been transferred to Pope's Army of Virginia. Be that as it may, they would stand steady against the decimating fire of Hood's Brigade on 30 August, the decisive second day at Manassas.

Another veteran of Union organization, the 2nd Wisconsin, had received their baptism of fire during the First Battle of Manassas. On 28 August, when Jackson unleashed his men near Brawner's Farm, these men from the Badger State were sent forward in response, being the only regiment in John Gibbon's brigade that faced the opening Confederate volleys to have combat experience. Even then, their diminutive colonel, Edgar O'Connor, must have wondered how his command would react. Since the less than stellar Union performance at First Manassas over a year earlier, they had spent most of their time in camp drilling. "The little colonel", as he was known by some of his troops, had no reason to fear a repeat of the earlier battle, however, his men stood firm in the face of the serried ranks of the 5,000 men of Taliaferro's entire division.

CONFEDERATE TROOPS

The Wisconsin men of "The Black Hat Brigade" waited for the advancing Southerners to come into range, little knowing their opponents had far more combat experience. Their foes were Jackson's stalwart "foot cavalry", whose first taste of combat had also been at First Manassas. They

William Wallace would be promoted to colonel of the 18th South Carolina after the regiment's commanding officer was killed at Second Manassas. This photograph was taken several years later, because Wallace is depicted as brigadier general, a rank he attained in September 1864. His double-breasted frock coat was of the style preferred by many Confederate officers. USAMHI

had gained more combat experience during the Valley Campaign, and the "Stonewall Brigade" (a designation that would not become official until 30 May 1863) had paid the price for their marching and determined fighting, becoming ragged in the process. Their mixed uniforms were threadbare, shoes worn, and rations monotonous and at times sparse. Yet these soldiers were the backbone of Jackson's wing (or corps as it would later be designated).

Most were from rural backgrounds, as were a great number of Confederate fighting men, and were drawn from some 18 counties in the Shenandoah Valley. Thus, they literally were campaigning in their own backyards. Rigid training under Jackson, strict military discipline and unshakable self-belief welded them into a formidable force. They, along with James Longstreet's infantry, were more than a match for Pope's troops as they maneuvered during the summer of 1862.

Although the core of the Army of Northern Virginia was foot soldiers, Robert E. Lee's command also boasted some fine artillery batteries. Once again the men tended to come from nearby locales, and as a result had a common bond helping build unit cohesion. Some of the organizations had existed as militia before the war, which meant that their members also boasted considerable expertise as gunners.

Lee, likewise, was fortunate enough to have at his disposal some of the finest cavalry to fight on either side during the war. Southerners counted within their number numerous well-mounted and experienced equestrians. In fact, during the early part of the war Confederate horse soldiers generally proved to be more adept then their Union counterparts; performing reconnaissance and raids they became the eyes and ears of Lee's army. One of these men particularly gained fame for his exploits. A youthful Virginia-born cavalier by the name of James Ewell Brown Stuart had graduated from West Point just a little over six years before the war. Despite his junior status, he had been made a lieutenant colonel early in the conflict, and not long after participating in actions at Harpers Ferry and the Battle of First Manassas he rose to the rank of brigadier general. Flamboyant and brave, "Jeb" Stuart garnered further laurels during the Peninsula and Seven Days operations, leading to his promotion to major general on 25 July 1862, when he took command of all of the Army of Northern Virginia's cavalry. Stuart's daring leadership would plague Pope's forces in the field during that summer, although he himself was caught napping on the eve of Second Manassas, and barely escaped capture by Union cavalrymen.

CEDAR MOUNTAIN, 9 AUGUST 1862

Major General Joseph Hooker, seen here as a brigadier general, led the 2nd Division of Heintzelman's III Corps. He would meet the enemy at Kettle Run, two days before Second Manassas, and displayed an aggressive nature that helped win him the nickname "Fighting Joe". NA

On 14 July, Pope started an advance toward Gordonsville. With about 80,000 troops around Richmond, Lee had McClellan's army of 90,000 in front of him and Pope's 50,000 converging from the north. Faced with the certainty of eventual defeat unless he seized the initiative, Lee took advantage of McClellan's inactivity and sent Jackson north toward Gordonsville with 12,000 men, among other things to defend the vital Virginia Central Railroad, which connected the Valley with Richmond. On Jackson's request, Lee next sent A.P. Hill with reinforcements, raising Jackson's available manpower to 24,000.

At the same time, Federal forces made their way slowly toward Culpeper, Virginia. Jackson was delighted to learn that it was Banks, his old adversary from the Valley Campaign, who was heading his way. Jackson decided to strike rapidly toward the vicinity of Culpeper to destroy the first enemy corps to arrive, reasoning he would, thereafter, be able to operate from a central position and defeat the other two corps in detail.

Jackson's Corps was rested, their mounts in good shape, and the men had great confidence in their leaders, while they themselves were in the main battle-wise veterans. These factors and the confidence born of previous victories, made this force the best that Jackson had fielded to date. Morale was high. Jackson had every reason to think he would again carry the day. Despite his reputation for rapid marches his progress was slow, in great part because of the confusion caused once again by his penchant for keeping his plans to himself. Despite Lee's urging to maintain good communications with his subordinates, Jackson once more failed to convey his overall blueprint to his division commanders – Charles Winder, Richard "Bald Head" Ewell, and A.P. Hill. They did not know their superior's original intentions much less his subsequent modifications.

On 8 August this flaw in leadership led to chaos along the march route. Jackson had changed the order of march, and sent Ewell by an alternative route to Culpeper. This resulted in Ewell's and Hill's troops becoming entangled as the two elements crossed. Perturbed by Jackson's refusal to share his aims, Hill did little to disentangle the two columns. This meant that by day's end his units had moved only about two miles, while Ewell's men tramped only eight miles, rather than the 20 the force was supposed to make. The ability to march an army, being as much a part of generalship as actually directing the men in combat, the Confederates made a poor show.

Nevertheless, on the next day Hill woke his troops early and quickly had them on the road to make up for the lost time of the previous day. He caught up with Winder, who in turn was not far behind Ewell. As such, it was Ewell's vanguard that made first contact with Banks's advance force.

Shortly after noon some of his men ran into the Union cavalry, with a few of their guns in support on a low ridge planted with corn. Sizing

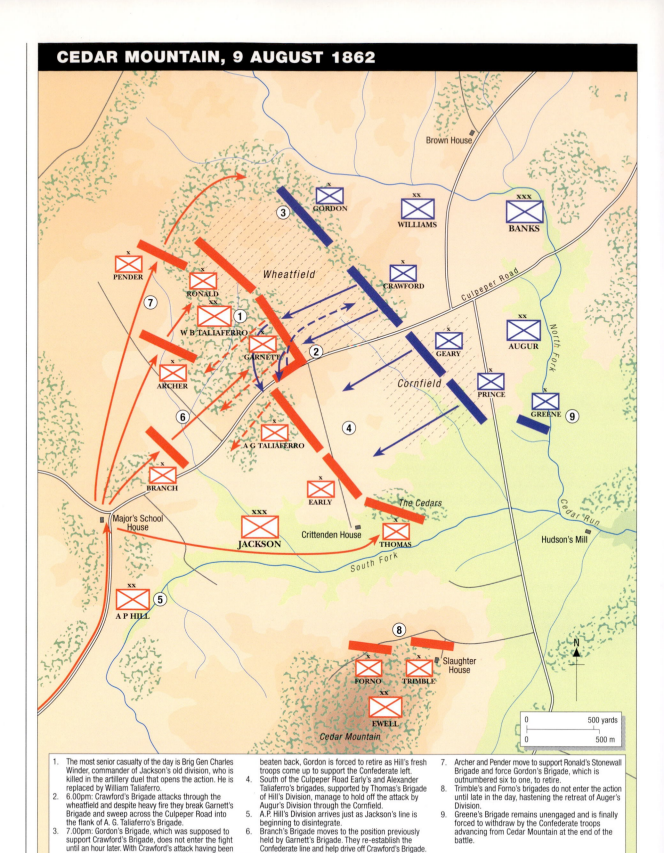

CEDAR MOUNTAIN, 9 AUGUST 1862

Brown House

GORDON · WILLIAMS · BANKS

PENDER · RONALD · W B TALIAFERRO · GARNETT · *Wheatfield* · CRAWFORD · *Culpeper Road* · GEARY · AUGUR

ARCHER · PRINCE · *Cornfield* · GREENE

A G TALIAFERRO

BRANCH · EARLY · *The Cedars*

Major's School House · JACKSON · Crittenden House · THOMAS · Hudson's Mill

South Fork · *Cedar Run*

A P HILL

FORNO · TRIMBLE · Slaughter House

EWELL

Cedar Mountain

N

| 0 | 500 yards |
| 0 | 500 m |

1. The most senior casualty of the day is Brig Gen Charles Winder, commander of Jackson's old division, who is killed in the artillery duel that opens the action. He is replaced by William Taliaferro.

2. 6.00pm: Crawford's Brigade attacks through the wheatfield and despite heavy fire they break Garnett's Brigade and sweep across the Culpeper Road into the flank of A. G. Taliaferro's Brigade.

3. 7.00pm: Gordon's Brigade, which was supposed to support Crawford's Brigade, does not enter the fight until an hour later. With Crawford's attack having been beaten back, Gordon is forced to retire as Hill's fresh troops come up to support the Confederate left.

4. South of the Culpeper Road Early's and Alexander Taliaferro's brigades, supported by Thomas's Brigade of Hill's Division, manage to hold off the attack by Augur's Division through the Cornfield.

5. A.P. Hill's Division arrives just as Jackson's line is beginning to disintegrate.

6. Branch's Brigade moves to the position previously held by Garnett's Brigade. They re-establish the Confederate line and help drive off Crawford's Brigade.

7. Archer and Pender move to support Ronald's Stonewall Brigade and force Gordon's Brigade, which is outnumbered six to one, to retire.

8. Trimble's and Forno's brigades do not enter the action until late in the day, hastening the retreat of Auger's Division.

9. Greene's Brigade remains unengaged and is finally forced to withdraw by the Confederate troops advancing from Cedar Mountain at the end of the battle.

up the situation, Jackson formulated his plan. He ordered a large artillery force into position on both flanks of the advancing infantry. Ewell's command was to hook around the Union's eastern flank across the slopes of Cedar Mountain. Winder was told to go to the left while Hill remained in reserve.

It took time for the troops to deploy, but eventually Confederate artillery opened up. But the bombardment had an unsuspected consequence. Crossfire from Ewell's batteries actually inhibited his advance at first. Even worse, Winder suffered a mortal wound not long after the fighting began.

Banks chose this moment to attack, his troops striking Jackson's center and left. With Winder's Division disrupted by the loss of their commander the Federals overwhelmed Garnett's Brigade and threatened to roll up Jackson's line. Every regimental commander in the brigade was killed or wounded and Winder's guns were withdrawn.

At that point Ewell attacked, Hill committed the reserves, and Jackson intervened personally to stabilize the line. Both sides of the Union line were outflanked. As the full moon rose, the Yankees retreated while their cavalry provided a screen. But Jackson had mismanaged the whole affair. His victory had been costly.

Ambrose P. Hill commanded a division in Jackson's right wing. Despite some confusion in reaching his position, Hill's forces were to play a key part in the Second Manassas clash. NA

PLAYING FOR TIME, 10–27 AUGUST 1862

Nonetheless, the battle of Cedar Mountain, as General Lee stated in his after action report, "effectually checked the progress of the enemy for the time … " Lee knew pressure from Washington would build, forcing Pope to advance. As early as 14 August, when Jesse Reno's arrival increased Pope's strength to 50,000, he made for the Rapidan with the intention of crossing his army at the historic Raccoon Ford, where "Mad" Anthony Wayne led his Pennsylvania brigade to reinforce the Marquis de Lafayette in 1781. On 13 August, in anticipation of this move, Lee ordered Longstreet's division with its two brigades under John B. Hood to move to Gordonsville. R.H. Anderson followed him, pre-empting by a day McClellan's movement from Harrison's landing toward Fort Monroe, Virginia. At the same time Jeb Stuart was ordered to move the main body of his cavalry toward Orange Court House, covering Longstreet's right.

Former US dragoon officer Richard S. "Dick" Ewell also headed a division in Jackson's wing. His men participated in the Cedar Mountain fight, as well as at Groveton, and Second Manassas. He lost his leg as a result of a wound sustained at Brawner's Farm. NA

Longstreet's troops reached the neighborhood of Gordonsville on the 16 August. The same day, Jackson quietly brought his command up behind the Clark's Mountain range, east of Orange Court House, to cover the Raccoon and Somerville fords of the Rapidan.

Lee followed and joined his army in Orange near the middle of August. On 19 August, he ordered his commanders to move against Pope and defeat him before McClellan could link up with the Army of Virginia. Longstreet advised a movement to the left in order to strike Pope's right. Lee and Jackson thought it better to turn Pope's left and put the Army of Northern Virginia between the Union troops and Washington. This would cut both Pope's line of supplies and retreat. To accomplish this, Lee directed Longstreet to cross the Rapidan at Raccoon Ford with the right wing of the army. He was to move toward Culpeper Court House, while Jackson, with the left wing, was to cross at

Confederate Major General John Bell Hood did double duty under Longstreet, serving as both a division and brigade commander. NA

Somerville Ford and proceed in the same direction, keeping on Longstreet's left. R.H. Anderson's division and S.D. Lee's battalion of artillery was to follow Jackson, while Stuart, crossing at Morton's Ford, was to reach the Rappahannock by way of Stevensburg. He was directed to destroy the railroad bridge, cut Pope's communications, and operate on Longstreet's right.

Ever spoiling for a fight, Jackson wanted to attack earlier. Longstreet rebutted that he was not prepared. In addition, Fitz Hugh Lee's Brigade of Stuart's cavalry, the lead brigade on the march from Richmond, had strayed too far to the right, in the direction of Fredericksburg, and was a day late in joining the army, causing another delay.

During all this activity Stuart had set out with his small staff in search of Fitz Lee. On the evening of 17 August the group reached Verdiersville. Not finding his cavalry reinforcement waiting there as expected, Stuart dispatched a rider with a message for the troops to hurry to join him. He then had his horse unsaddled while he stripped off his saber belt, hat, and other gear to get a night's sleep in the garden of the Rhodes house.

Dawn of 18 August broke with the sound of hooves, which Stuart thought must be Fitz Lee. But it was not. Pope had called for a reconnaissance in the area, and Colonel Thorton Broadhead with elements of the 1st Michigan Cavalry along with the 5th New York had obliged. Now the blue-clad troopers were riding towards the slumbering "Beauty" Stuart. The Confederate cavalier jumped on his unsaddled horse and beat a quick retreat, leaving behind his tack, cloak, and sash. Also abandoned was his plumed hat, which he had recently received from a former comrade from his days in the United States Army, Samuel Crawford. After Cedar Mountain, Crawford and Stuart had met during a brief truce and the Confederate cavalryman bet his old friend that the Northern press would declare the clash a Union victory, which it was not. When the action was reported as Stuart predicted, Crawford sent the hat to Stuart in payment of his wager. Although leaving behind many personal items, Stuart managed to vault the fence on his steed and escaped capture.

Stone Bridge across Bull Run Creek was in ruins after the first engagement fought there, as evidenced by this March 1862 photograph. Finding fords and repairing or building new bridges were all part of the game for the advancing Union troops as they sought an elusive Jackson. NA

28

His adjutant general, Major Norman R. Fitz Hugh, however, was not that fortunate. He fell into the hands of the Union troops. What was worse, the major had a copy of Lee's order of march, and had no time to dispose of it before capture. These documents were quickly forwarded to Pope, who hastened to evacuate Culpeper and put the Rappahannock between himself and Lee.

Lee's original plan now had to be revised. He would march his 50,000 men at dawn of 20 August, but not against Culpeper Court House. Instead, Longstreet marched to Kelly's Ford of the Rappahannock, while Jackson marched by way of Stevensburg and Brandy Station toward Rappahannock

Bridge, bivouacking for the night near Stevensburg. Stuart, with Beverly Robertson's cavalry brigade, had a spirited contest that day with George Bayard's cavalry, near Brandy Station. Forced from that point, Bayard took position between Brandy Station and Rappahannock Bridge, still guarding the Federal rear, from which position Stuart again routed him and drove him across the Rappahannock, under cover of Pope's batteries on the high northern bank. The Confederates captured 64 prisoners and lost 16 killed and wounded.

The morning of 21 August found Lee on the south bank of the Rappahannock, with Jackson on the left, extended from the Rappahannock Station railroad bridge to Beverly's Ford. Robertson's 5th Virginia Cavalry had made a dash there, scattering the Federal infantry nearby, disabling a battery, and spending most of the day on the north side of the river aided by Jackson's batteries on the south side. On the approach of a large Federal force, Thomas L. Rosser, under Stuart's orders, recrossed. Longstreet extended Lee's line from Rappahannock Bridge to Kelly's Ford. Pope's 55,000 men held the commanding ground on the north bank of the Rappahannock. Likewise, a lively artillery duel was maintained during the day between the confronting armies, but with little or no damage to either.

The open terrain here dictated caution; strategic movements could not be concealed. It was evident that Pope's army was not vulnerable to a frontal assault. Also, his left was difficult to approach. The fact that he received reinforcements steadily from the direction of Fredericksburg was of consequence too.

Accordingly, in conference with Jackson, Lee determined to turn Pope's right, a move that would place the Confederates in his rear, cutting him off from the old highway that led through the Piedmont country, through Warrenton toward Washington. Moreover, Lee could use the Bull Run mountains to screen his movements.

These ruins of the railroad bridge at Blackburn's Ford are typical of the damage inflicted during the efforts made by both sides to disrupt the enemy's lines of communications. LC

The railroad bridge near Union Mills remained intact, allowing Federal rolling stock to continue along this section of the Orange & Alexandria. LC

LEFT **The Rebels had not destroyed this bridge, which spanned the Hazel River, a tributary of the Rappahannock. LC**

BELOW **Yet more of the handiwork of Union engineers is evident, in this case a bridge provided by men of McDowell's Corps just four days before the battle. LC**

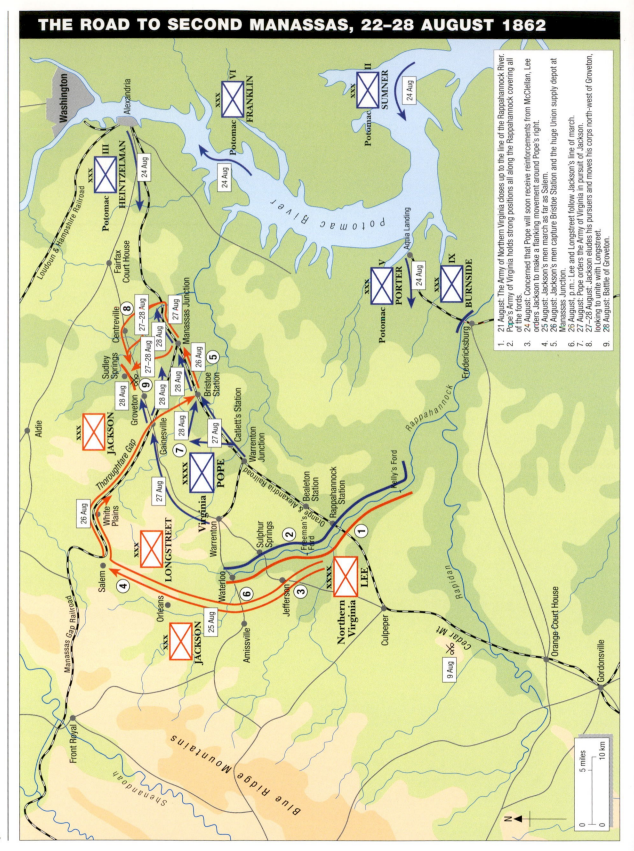

THE ROAD TO SECOND MANASSAS, 22–28 AUGUST 1862

Washington

Alexandria

Potomac
HEINTZELMAN
xxx III

24 Aug

24 Aug

Potomac
FRANKLIN
xxx VI

Potomac
SUMNER
xxx II

24 Aug

Loudoun & Hampshire Railroad

Potomac River

Fairfax
Court House

Aquia Landing

Potomac
PORTER
xxx V

xxx IX
BURNSIDE

24 Aug

Centreville

8

27–28 Aug

27–28 Aug

27–28 Aug

28 Aug

27 Aug

Sudley
Springs

28 Aug

9

28 Aug

28 Aug

Groveton

28 Aug

26 Aug

Manassas Junction

5

Bristoe
Station

JACKSON
xxx

Gainesville

7

28 Aug

27 Aug

Catlett's Station

Thoroughfare Gap

Warrenton
Junction

White Plains

26 Aug

Aldie

27 Aug

Virginia
POPE
xxxx

Orange & Alexandria Railroad

Fredericksburg

Rappahannock

LONGSTREET
xxx

Salem

4

Warrenton

Sulphur
Springs

2

Bealeton
Station

Freeman's Ford

Rappahannock
Station

Kelly's Ford

1

Manassas Gap Railroad

Orleans

JACKSON
xxx

25 Aug

Amissville

Waterloo

6

Jefferson

3

Northern
Virginia
LEE
xxxx

Culpeper

Cedar Mt

9 Aug

Rapidan

Orange Court House

Gordonsville

Front Royal

Shenandoah

Blue Ridge Mountains

1. 21 August: The Army of Northern Virginia closes up to the line of the Rappahannock River.
2. Pope's Army of Virginia holds strong positions all along the Rappahannock covering all of the fords.
3. 24 August: Concerned that Pope will soon receive reinforcements from McClellan, Lee orders Jackson to make a flanking movement around Pope's right.
4. 25 August: Jackson's men march as far as Salem.
5. 26 August: Jackson's men capture Bristoe Station and the huge Union supply depot at Manassas Junction.
6. 26 August, p.m.: Lee and Longstreet follow Jackson's line of march.
7. 27 August: Pope orders the Army of Virginia in pursuit of Jackson.
8. 27–28 August: Jackson eludes his pursuers and moves his corps north-west of Groveton, looking to unite with Longstreet.
9. 28 August: Battle of Groveton.

N

0   5 miles
0   10 km

34

Supplying the Federal forces in the field required a network of wagons and railroads. Union operations in enemy country taxed both combat soldiers and logistical support personnel. USAMHI

Fresh beef for a famished Federal army sometimes came on the hoof – as evidenced by this photograph of a herd crossing a bridge on its way toward hungry troops. In comparison to his Southern adversary, the Northern soldier had ample sustenance during the campaign. USAMHI

The first step in this strategic envelopment was to mobilize the left wing of his army under Jackson, behind the protective screen of the mountain ranges, without Pope's knowledge. While Jackson and Stuart drew Pope's attention along the Rappahannock, north of the railroad, Lee moved Longstreet from his right, by concealed roads, and placed him in Jackson's rear. This left Jackson free to fall back after dark so he could march to a position further up the river, but still maintain contact with Longstreet's left.

This was accomplished during the night of 21/22 August. That day, preceded by cavalry, Jackson reached the neighborhood of Sulphur Springs, where the great highway, from Culpeper Court House toward Washington, crossed the Rappahannock and then passed through

Warrenton to Centreville. Simultaneously, Longstreet, through vigorous use of skirmishers and artillery, maintained Pope's attention, causing him to reinforce his position at Beverly's Ford, in the expectation that Longstreet would try to force a passage there and attack his center. Jackson's line of march was harassed by cavalry and infantry from a detached column that Pope was moving up the north bank of the river, to keep pace with whatever movement Lee might be making to his left.

At about noon an especially bold encounter ensued at Freeman's Ford as Jackson's rear was passing that point. His rearguard, under Isaac R. Trimble, deployed and awaited the Federal attack. Hood, with two of Longstreet's brigades, came up at about 4.00pm, when Trimble, aided by these reinforcements, launched a spirited attack on the Federal brigade, which had forded the river. Trimble drove back the Union troops in confusion. A third crossing, in pursuit of information, was made by Confederate cavalry, infantry, and artillery at Fant's Ford, but they soon retired, having gained little intelligence from this reconnaissance.

Elsewhere, when Jackson reached the river opposite Sulphur Springs, and found the ford unguarded, he at once began moving his troops to the other side. He sent over the 13th Georgia and two batteries, while Jubal Early crossed, on an old mill dam, about a mile further down the river. It began raining while these troops crossed, and an afternoon of showers was followed by a night of heavy downpour and darkness, preventing the crossing of more men. By morning the swollen river was unfordable and Jackson's advance guard under Early was isolated on the opposite shore.

Pope's main body continued to hold its position, near the railway, on 22 August, as he was unwilling to move farther from his expected reinforcements from Fredericksburg. Fearing an attack from Longstreet, whose whereabouts remained unknown to him, Pope did not move to his right to intercept Jackson's forces.

During the morning Lee dispatched Stuart with the main body of his cavalry to Waterloo Bridge, four miles above Warrenton Springs. There, Stuart, with 1,500 men and two guns, crossed the river and began a rapid march for Pope's rear, to break the railway leading to Washington and gather information, in a similar manner to his grand ride around

McClellan at Richmond earlier in the year. With a good road to march on, he reached Warrenton unopposed. After halting there for a short rest, he continued eastward via Auburn Mills to Catlett's Station on the Orange & Alexandria Railroad. He intended to destroy the bridge over Cedar Creek near that place. The downpour that had swelled the Rappahannock caught Stuart, and he reached his objective in the midst of rain and darkness. In the process, his troopers had captured a fleeing black man, who led Stuart to a camp where they seized Pope's headquarters wagons.

Stuart quickly captured the Federal commander's staff, his personal baggage, and official papers. Despite gaining these prizes, Stuart's efforts to destroy the wagon trains and the railroad bridge only partially succeeded. The rain and the darkness made it impossible for him to carry out his orders completely, so he began his return before daylight on 23 August with 300 prisoners. Recrossing the Rappahannock in the evening of the same day, he withdrew without further incident. He had taught Pope a lesson on the subject of rear guards, and caused some concern among Federal troops as to the safety of their lines of retreat. Additionally, Stuart had captured correspondence between Pope and Halleck, which provided Lee with a concise picture of the strength and the plans of his antagonist.

Meanwhile, the heavy evening rain of 22 August interrupted Jackson's movement and compelled Lee to temporarily abandon his intended flanking activities. Jackson repaired the bridge at the springs in order to extricate Early, who was still on the north bank of the Rappahannock.

Pope, knowing the river was impassable, gave up his scheme of crossing to attack Lee's rear. He was now determined to concentrate against the Confederates on the north side of the river. Early on the morning of 23 August he ordered Sigel toward Sulphur Springs, by way of Fayetteville, followed by Banks and Reno. McDowell, on Pope's left, received orders to burn the railroad bridge at Rappahannock Station, which to that point he had kept intact, and move toward Warrenton.

This would put him in a position to oppose any movement of Lee from Sulphur Springs toward Warrenton. John Reynolds' Division of 6,000 men, from Aquia Creek followed McDowell.

With Union forces on the move Early maintained a bullish facade while awaiting the reconstruction of the bridge in his rear. He held the road against the advance of Sigel's 25,000 men, who Pope had ordered forward to crush the Confederates on the north side of the river. Sigel believed that Lee's whole army was in front of him, however, and merely indulged in skirmishing and artillery fire until dark, after which he went into camp and advised Pope to withdraw his corps to a better position.

In the meantime, Ewell crossed the river to consult with Early during the night. They decided, in view of the large force before him, that it was not expedient to bring on a battle at that place. Orders were given at 3.00am for Early to withdraw, which he did soon after daylight, moving his men to Jackson's rear.

At about 10.00pm on 23 August, Pope himself, accompanied by McDowell's Corps and Reynolds's Division, reached Warrenton. At that time more than 50,000 men of the Army of Virginia had concentrated along the turnpike between Jackson at Sulphur Springs and Warrenton. By the next morning Pope was preparing to destroy Lee, whom he supposed was still north of the Rappahannock, as Sigel had reported. To gather more intelligence John Buford's cavalry was sent to Waterloo to reconnoiter and to destroy the bridge over the Rappahannock at that point. This would also permit him to slip behind Lee's supposed position. Sigel, Banks, and Reno were to move toward the same point, from opposite Sulphur Springs, while McDowell was placed along the roads leading to Sulphur Springs and to Waterloo to support the movement. As Sigel approached the river, A.P. Hill opened up his batteries and an artillery engagement ensued. Thus, Sigel cautiously continued his march up the river stung by Hill's batteries. It was well into the afternoon before Buford learned that there were no Confederates on the north side of the Rappahannock.

ABOVE **Union troops charging Jackson's left flank on 9 August 1862 met stiff resistance. LC**

LEFT **Days later, after the stinging combat had ended, Union men could remove their jackets and coats in the summer heat and humidity to relax, at least those who were fortunate enough to have survived Cedar Mountain. LC**

Sigel took most of 24 August to cover the six miles from Sulphur Springs to Waterloo, where he arrived late in the afternoon. Once on the scene he found the Confederates on the south side of the river, but holding and defending the bridge. The continuing thunder of Lee's guns had thoroughly engaged Sigel's concentration during the entire day. This was exactly as Lee had intended, as he wished to divert attention from the new flank movement that he had already begun.

Nor did Pope have any idea of what was transpiring. In the afternoon, after learning that there were no Confederates north of the Rappahannock, he communicated with Halleck that he would "early to-morrow … move back a considerable part of my force to the neighborhood of Rappahannock station … " Apparently concerned by his lack of information about Longstreet, he wanted to regroup his own forces while considering what to do next.

Still desiring to strike a telling blow at Pope before McClellan's main body could reach him, Lee ordered divisions from Richmond under John C. Walker, Lafayette McLaws and D.H. Hill, which had been withheld as a safeguard in case McClellan attempted another assault on the capital. Lee and Jackson devised a plan of attack by which the latter would move rapidly to Pope's rear, cut his line of communication at Bristoe Station, destroy the Federal depot at Manassas Junction, then fall back to the north of the Warrenton Turnpike. There, he was to await the arrival of Lee with Longstreet's Wing. In turn, Longstreet would remain one more day on the banks of the Rappahannock to detain and confuse Pope.

During the night of 24 August, Longstreet's men took the place of Jackson opposite Sulphur Springs, allowing Jackson to begin his march early on the morning of 25 August. Leaving their baggage train behind and taking only ambulances and ordnance wagons with them, Jackson's men once more traveled light, leaving behind their knapsacks and carrying three days' cooked rations in their haversacks. Confident of being able to supply his men from the enemy's stores, Jackson was once again on the prowl.

Leaving Jeffersonton, Jackson headed north-west along the great highway leading to the Valley by way of Chester Gap. His sun-bronzed veterans were elated by the conviction that they were again bound for the scene of their victories of the preceding spring. But a short distance beyond Amissville, they changed course, turning from the north-west to the north-east. Jackson's column pressed steadily forward through the long August day, without halt, until they had covered 25 miles and reached the vicinity of Salem, on the Manassas Gap Railroad, just as the sun sank behind the ridge to their left.

At dawn on 26 August, Jackson's men were again puzzled to find themselves marching to the south-east, following the line of the Manassas Gap Railroad, through Thoroughfare Gap to Gainesville, where Stuart joined them with his cavalry and led the way from that hamlet directly to Bristoe Station. They reached there near dark, after a march of 24 miles, without having met opposition. Jackson and his 22,000 "foot cavalry" and Stuart with his intrepid troopers were now in Pope's rear.

They immediately proceeded to destroy everything in their path, while capturing trains moving toward Washington and breaking up detached Federal encampments along the railroad. Jackson then sent Trimble's Brigade of infantry and Stuart with a portion of his cavalry, through the darkness, four miles further to Manassas Junction, which they reached and captured after brief resistance at about midnight.

Weary from their rapid marches made on short rations, Jackson's fatigued and famished soldiers looked in disbelief at the mountains of supplies of every description they found piled high at Manassas.

This same day, Lee and Longstreet, leaving 6,000 men at Waterloo to guard the trains, followed Jackson marching as far as Orleans. Apprised of these various movements by his scouts and spies, but failing to comprehend their destination or purpose, Pope issued orders that scattered, rather than concentrated, his large army. He first ordered a concentration on Warrenton; Fitz John Porter with 10,000 men reached Bealeton, and Samuel F. Heintzelman with his 10,000 men reached Warrenton Junction on their way to obey this order. The corps from McClellan's army under Edwin V. Sumner, William B. Franklin, and Jacob D. Cox were that day marching toward Pope from Alexandria. Late in the night Pope again changed his orders, directing his troops to march on Gainesville, to intercept what he supposed would be Jackson's line of retreat from Manassas. Different portions of his command were now headed in that direction, but all were hindered by a confusion of orders and a resulting mixing of marching columns.

On 27 August, Lee rode with Longstreet through Salem and the Plains station. On the ride, an attack of a small body of Federal cavalry came near to capturing General Lee. Likewise, in the early morning Jackson marched the divisions of William B. Taliaferro (previously under Charles Winder, killed at Cedar Mountain) and of A.P. Hill to Manassas Junction, where they rested and joined in the feasting on the vast stores of quartermaster and commissary supplies that the Federals had gathered at this important depot. Ewell was left behind, at Bristoe, to protect Jackson's rear and oppose any advance from the line of the Rappahannock. There, in the afternoon, he fought a vigorous engagement with Porter, repulsing him before withdrawing across Broad Run. Late in the day Ewell's column continued to Manassas Junction. The storm clouds of the approaching battle were beginning to gather.

BRAWNER'S FARM AND THOROUGHFARE GAP, 28 AUGUST 1862

When Jackson began his withdrawal from Manassas on the evening of 27 August, which included the wholesale destruction of whatever his men could not carry off, he marched north toward Centreville and other sites along the Warrenton Pike. This would make it more difficult for Pope to cut him off from the approaching Longstreet. By the next morning, Jackson reported that he made immediate disposition of his command based upon the belief that the Union main body "was leaving the road and inclining toward Manassas Junction." Thus, in his own words, he advanced his command "through the woods, leaving Groveton on the left, until it reached a commanding position near Brawner's house [the residence of a local farmer named John Brawner]."

Jackson's guess about Pope's plans proved correct. He had indeed directed the Army of Virginia to converge upon Manassas Junction, where he believed the Confederates were in position. A brief fracas with some of Sigel's troops on the morning of 28 August confirmed Jackson's suspicions. During the fight, Captain George Gaither's troop of the 1st Virginia Cavalry managed to capture a courier, who carried the order of march for the Union forces dictated by Pope. Jackson knew what his enemy had in mind – the same could not be said of Pope.

In fact, Sigel had captured some Confederate prisoners as well, but the information they gave misleadingly indicated Jackson was still at Manassas. In reality the men of William Taliaferro's Division were concealed in the woods north of Groveton, with another division under

In the aftermath of Cedar Mountain, local citizens, such as the Robinson family, who owned this home, could return to their precarious lives. USAMHI

BATTLE OF GROVETON, 28 AUGUST 1862

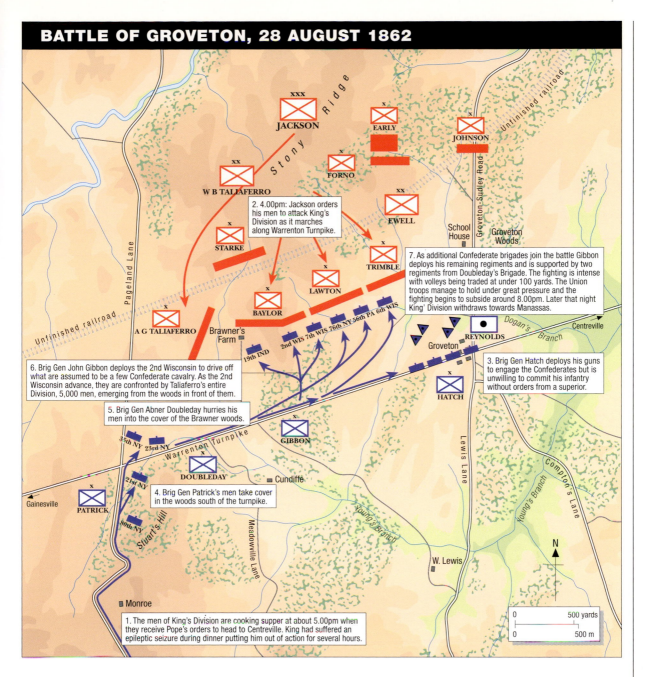

2. 4.00pm: Jackson orders his men to attack King's Division as it marches along Warrenton Turnpike.

7. As additional Confederate brigades join the battle Gibbon deploys his remaining regiments and is supported by two regiments from Doubleday's Brigade. The fighting is intense with volleys being traded at under 100 yards. The Union troops manage to hold under great pressure and the fighting begins to subside around 8.00pm. Later that night King' Division withdraws towards Manassas.

3. Brig Gen Hatch deploys his guns to engage the Confederates but is unwilling to commit his infantry without orders from a superior.

6. Brig Gen John Gibbon deploys the 2nd Wisconsin to drive off what are assumed to be a few Confederate cavalry. As the 2nd Wisconsin advance, they are confronted by Taliaferro's entire Division, 5,000 men, emerging from the woods in front of them.

5. Brig Gen Abner Doubleday hurries his men into the cover of the Brawner woods.

4. Brig Gen Patrick's men take cover in the woods south of the turnpike.

1. The men of King's Division are cooking supper at about 5.00pm when they receive Pope's orders to head to Centreville. King had suffered an epileptic seizure during dinner putting him out of action for several hours.

Richard S. Ewell heading toward Stone Bridge, and A.P. Hill's Light Division moving westward from Centreville towards the Groveton area.

Late in the afternoon with Jackson's men out of sight in the woods, a Federal column marched onto the scene. Brigadier General John F. Reynolds's Division was in the vanguard, and engaged in a brief clash with a Southern screening detachment. The action was brief and Reynolds continued on toward Manassas Junction, not realizing the Confederates were concealed nearby.

Following behind came Rufus King's Division at around 5.00pm. A little earlier, McDowell had been with King, but had departed in search of Pope to confer with his superior. King was thus the senior officer although he

LEFT **Given the number of troops who fell on 9 August the Confederate name for the battle, Slaughter Mountain, was appropriate. But it was the home of Reverend Slaughter, who lived on the mountain that was the source of the name.**

BELOW **The Confederates lost 1,418 troops killed or wounded at Cedar Mountain, including Brigadier General Charles S. Winder, who led Jackson's 1st Division. Winder breathed his last in this rustic residence. USAMHI**

was unwell, having recently suffered an epileptic seizure. Unfortunately, he would be debilitated by another attack later that evening.

Unaware of their commander's condition, the division proceeded along the turnpike, with the 1st Rhode Island Cavalry riding point for the lead brigade under John P. Hatch. The cavalrymen noticed nothing unusual, nor did the 14th Brooklyn, a zouave unit that Hatch sent out as flankers to guard against surprise attack. They, too, failed to detect the enemy waiting in numbers to spring an ambush.

Stonewall had placed three batteries in front of William E. Starke's brigade above the village of Groveton along Stony Ridge. Jackson told his division commanders Ewell and Taliaferro "Bring up your men, gentlemen!" In short order, the Virginia gunners of Captain Asher Garber's Staunton Artillery began to fire over the heads of Confederate skirmishers. The gates of Hell had opened; Manassas would once again be the arena for a bloody struggle between North and South.

Garber's artillerists had the Federals targeted after only three rounds. They were soon joined by the other two batteries, causing the Union troops to sprint for cover. Hatch ordered up one of his own batteries, Battery L, 1st New York Light Artillery, captained by John Reynolds. The six 3-in. ordnance rifles took position north-west of the scattering of half a dozen simple buildings that made up Groveton. Men of the 24th New York Infantry rapidly dismantled a fence obstructing the field of fire, allowing Reynolds to bring his pieces to bear.

The Yankees were outgunned though, as George Breck, a lieutenant in the outfit indicated. Breck wrote: "The shot and shell fell and burst in our midst every minute, exploding in the middle of the road between men and horses and caissons, throwing dirt and gravel all over us, and making it impossible for the cannoniers to man their pieces."

The Union buried 314 of their dead on the field, almost in the shadow of Cedar Mountain. In all 2,403 Union men were wounded, killed, or missing after the battle. LC

OVERLEAF **On 28 August at Brawner's Farm the untried 2nd, 6th, and 7th Wisconsin infantry regiments, and the 19th Indiana of BrigGen John Gibbon's "Black Hat Brigade" underwent their baptism of fire. Around 6.00pm they engaged what Gibbon believed to be a cavalry rearguard supported by artillery. Leading his men forward Gibbon soon realized that the Rebels were present in strength. His 2,100 Midwesterners faced Taliaferro's Division 6,200 strong. Before reinforcements could arrive, the Federal and Confederate forces had closed to within 75 yards of each other. The action continued until nightfall and Gibbon's units took 33 per cent casualties. The resolve displayed by Gibbon's men in this and later actions was soon to win them a new name as "The Iron Brigade" of the Union Army. (Mike Adams)**

During the pounding, Hatch's infantrymen remained frozen in place. Marsena Patrick's unblooded command, which brought up the rear of the column, likewise halted and sought protection in the woods to the south of the roadway. Another of King's brigades led by Abner Doubleday left the pike, too, and headed into the woods that stood on Brawner's farm.

Only Southern-born John Gibbon, who had three brothers in the Confederate forces took the fight to the enemy. After Gibbon's 6th Wisconsin, which marched at the head of his column, came under attack, he formed his men into a battleline. He also deployed the artillery of Captain Joseph Campbell's Battery B, 4th US Artillery.

Campbell's regulars unlimbered their 12-pdr Napoleons on high ground to the east of Brawner's farmstead.

In the meantime, without a corps or division commander to take charge, Gibbon rushed off to consult with Doubleday. The latter officer postulated that Jackson was in Centreville, and therefore the column only faced cavalry, who could be driven off with relative ease. With that Gibbon rode back to his men and launched his only veteran unit, the 2nd Wisconsin, against the Confederate artillery.

As the Federals advanced on the Southern guns, the 800 men of the veteran Stonewall Brigade emerged from the woods. The fighting was ferocious, with the two sides exchanging volleys at a scant 80 yds! Despite the devastating power of rifled musketry at this range, neither Union nor Confederate forces gave way. Confederate Brigadier General Taliaferro stated, "Out in the sunlight, in the dying daylight, and under the stars they stood, and although they could not advance, they would not retire."

Talaiferro further described the scene as "one of the most terrific engagements that can be conceived … " Confederate troops "held the farmhouse," he concluded, while "the enemy held the orchard. To the left our men stood in the open field without shelter of any kind." It appeared to Taliaferro like a painting depicting a moment of battle frozen in time. This surreal situation continued for some 20 minutes before the 19th Indiana came up to support the stalwart Wisconsin soldiers on their left. The commanding officer of the Hoosier troops, Colonel Solomon Meredith, captured the moment: "The enemy was secreted under cover of a fence and did not make their appearance until we had approached to within 75 yards. Immediately upon our halting the enemy fired. Three different times they came up at a charge, but the 19th stood firm." And each time the Confederates fell back to their fence line.

Meanwhile, on the right, Starke's Louisianians pressed the Federal troops. Jackson also sent nearly half of the Georgians from Lawton's Brigade to lengthen the Confederate line, but they met stiff opposition from the 7th Wisconsin, which Gibbon had added to his line. These blue-coated foot soldiers stood their ground, keeping the Southerners from moving forward, although the two forces remained but 100 yds apart.

The 6th Wisconsin, the last remaining regiment under Gibbon, also was sent to the front of Campbell's Battery. This regiment's commanding officer, Colonel Lysander Cutler, after learning that the 2nd Wisconsin was being slaughtered, and receiving the order to "join on the right of the 7th [Wisconsin] and engage the enemy," took his place in front of his command. Once in position, he called out, "Forward, guide center, march." In response, according to Major Rufus Dawes of the 6th, " … every man scrambled up the bank and over the fence, in the face of shot and shell … " Thus, by 6.45pm Gibbon's whole brigade was engaged in furious action.

Their adversaries clearly were not just a few Confederate cavalry troopers, but a strong force of infantry with substantial artillery support. There were six Southern brigades with 6,000 fighting men pitted against Gibbon's 2,100. Gibbon certainly needed urgent support, and made this known in a dispatch to divisional headquarters. When no response was forthcoming, Gibbon turned to the other brigade commanders. Again there was silence, except from Doubleday. To his credit, Doubleday did not stand by and watch the butchery. He sent two of his regiments, the

76th New York and the 56th Pennsylvania into the whirlwind. Still the battle raged. Colonel Dawes again depicted what he saw: "Through the intense smoke, through which we were advancing, I could see a blood red sun sinking behind the hills … The two crowds, they could not be called lines, were within, it seemed to me, fifty yards of each other, and they were pouring musketry into each other as rapidly as man can shoot."

Captain James S. Blain of the 26th Georgia Infantry knew what it was like to be on the receiving end of these volleys. He indicated the Georgians had been "ordered in just after dark." They "marched steadily across an open field for about 400 yards, over which the balls were flying by the thousands." Brigadier General Lawton was determined to press on. He ordered a charge. Captain Blain admitted: "The Yankees did fearful execution; men fell from the ranks by the dozens."

Undaunted, by 7.15pm Jackson decided to increase the intensity of the offensive. He had reserves from Ewell's command on hand, and Hill was approaching. He thought it was time for a head-on onslaught. This action fell to the 21st Georgia and the 21st North Carolina, known as the "Twin Twenty-ones", of Brigadier General Isaac Trimble's Brigade. They were ordered to assault the right of the Federal line, while Alexander Lawton's Brigade was to press the attack to their right, closer to the Union center.

Captain James F. Beal, who commanded a company of the 21st North Carolina, provided a Southern perspective on this stage of the fighting. He revealed that the Confederate infantrymen halted at a fence, which they quickly tore "down and piled the rails in front. It offered good protection." He went on to assert: "The Federals were in a gully, or branch about 100 yards distant. We opened fire on them, but it soon became so dark that we could not see their position, but could only fire at the flashes from their guns, as I suppose they would fire at ours."

Sergeant Uberton Burnham of the 76th New York Infantry provided a view of the engagement from the Northern ranks: "Waving their colors defiantly, the rebels advanced from the woods to charge upon Gibbon's

brigade to our left. Gibbon's men did not run. Those western men are not easily scared. They stood still and fired as fast as they could. We gave the Rebs a crossfire, thinning their ranks and prostrating their color bearer. The Rebels finding they were getting the worse of it turned their backs and pointed for the woods."

When Jackson did not achieve his aim on the right, the Union left became his next target. The gallant Confederate artilleryman John Pelham rushed his guns to within 100 yds of the 19th Indiana. Following Pelham's bombardment, the last three regiments in W.B. Taliaferro's Division, commanded by his uncle Colonel A.G. Taliaferro, advanced. Gibbon was forced to withdraw the 19th, but the Indianians were able to slow Taliaferro's Third Brigade. The attack ceased, as darkness and exhaustion brought an end to the fighting.

A private from the 2nd Wisconsin, Nathaniel Rollins, summed up the trying events of that 28 August. "Rebel infantry," he said, had "poured from the woods by the thousand." He continued: "For an hour and fifteen minutes the most terrific fire imaginable was kept up; the hill top, the valley, and the wooded side of the hill beyond was a continuous sheet of flame. Darkness came on, the stars came out, and still the bullets filled the air." By 9.00pm, however, Gibbon and Doubleday agreed that it was time to make an orderly withdrawal.

Gibbon's men in particular had performed admirably. The steely determination displayed in this and subsequent actions would earn his men the reputation as the "Iron Brigade" of the Northern armies. Despite the fact that they had been set upon without warning, the Federals sustained fewer casualties than the Confederates, with an estimated 1,000 dead and wounded.

The former Confederate facilities at Fort Beauregard provided the Union men with all the comforts of home, including a privy. Routine camp life would give way to campaigning once Pope took charge. USAMHI

Nevertheless, the Confederates gave a good account of themselves that evening, and during the course of the fighting some 1,250 had fallen, including nearly 40 per cent of Stonewall's seasoned brigade. This was a dreadful blow in all respects, as was the loss of Ewell, who having been wounded during the encounter, subsequently lost his leg to amputation. This put him out of action for some time, depriving Lee of one of his more pugnacious and dependable officers. William Taliaferro likewise was wounded. Because of this, William E. Starke was temporarily assigned command of the division, while Ewell's Division was placed under a Harvard-educated attorney named Alexander R. Lawton.

Both wounded divisional commanders had demonstrated short-comings during the action. Ewell had been slow in bringing his forces to the field and William Taliaferro had held back one of his brigades, and committed the others piecemeal.

Although Pope now knew the whereabouts of Jackson's wing, he seemed totally unconcerned as to the location and intentions of Longstreet's men. This oversight was to prove costly in the days to come.

In fact, Longstreet and Lee had halted at White Plains on the evening of 27 August. His column did not press forward with any great urgency despite Jackson's apparent vulnerability. Even on 28 August, Longstreet's forces did not break camp until 11.00am. to march toward Thoroughfare Gap. This was a rugged cut through the Bull Run Mountains that narrowed to as little as 100 yds in some places. Its north face was nearly perpendicular, with the south face less steep, but covered with tangles of ivy and boulders that provided excellent cover for anyone determined to hold the pass. Down the center ran a muddy stream from which rose walls of rock that measured several hundred feet in height.

Jackson had passed through the Gap on his march to Manassas, and it was an obvious route for the rest of the Army of Northern Virginia. Indeed, the Federals had received intelligence that Longstreet was marching on the Gap. As such, it seemed reasonable to expect this pass would be guarded by a strong Union force. On his own initiative, Major General McDowell ordered the 5,000 men of James B. Ricketts's 2nd Division to secure this vital pass, which was held only by the 1st New Jersey Cavalry.

McDowell's instincts were excellent, but Ricketts's command was no match for Longstreet's superior numbers. Even as he approached Thoroughfare Gap the New Jersey troopers were falling back, having been overwhelmed by the Southern advance.

Ricketts's response was to commit the 11th Pennsylvania Infantry, just as the Confederate 9th Georgia were setting up camp just east of the Gap. The Federal strike caught the Georgians by surprise, and the Pennsylvanians briefly gained the upper hand – that is until Brigadier General D.R. Jones sent forward a brigade from his division with another in support. Even then the Northerners did not yield and the arrival of the 13th Massachusetts helped bolster the line. Ricketts' men soon took up defensive positions, creating an impasse.

After dawdling for almost two days, Lee now became a dynamo. Colonel Evander Law's Brigade was sent scrambling over the rugged mountains on Ricketts' right, and C.M. Wilcox's Division was sent further north to Hopewell Gap in a bid to turn Ricketts's position. In addition, two regiments of Benning's Brigade had won a race with a detachment of 13th Massachusetts to seize the summit of Pond Mountain on the southern side of Thoroughfare Gap. Law's and Benning's men succeeded in flanking Ricketts's making his position untenable. He summarized the situation as follows: "The men moved forward gallantly but owing to the nature of the ground, the strongest positions being already held by the enemy, we were subjected to severe loss, without any prospect of gaining the gap." Even under these circumstances Ricketts's Division fought until darkness fell and then retired. At that point, nothing stood in Longstreet's path to Jackson.

Longstreet's move arguably constituted a major turning point for the Confederates. Not only did his breakthrough at Thoroughfare Gap allow him to combine with Jackson, but the fact that Pope seemed unaware of his presence had grave implications for the Army of Virginia.

Pope remained ignorant of Longstreet's approach as he took a late supper around 10.00pm on 28 August. While dining, news reached him of King's action at Groveton. He was delighted to learn that Jackson was still in the field, and was confident he could now bring the elusive Stonewall to bay. Pope dispatched orders for his commanders to concentrate their men at Groveton while King was to hold his ground to prevent Jackson escaping.

Although Pope intended King to maintain contact with Jackson, he learned that King had withdrawn to Manassas Junction at around 1.00am. A perturbed Pope issued new orders to his commanders around 5.00am on 29 August. These instructed McDowell to head toward Gainesville, taking King's men with him, while Sigel was to attack the enemy vigorously, pinning him in position. However, Pope's plan to surround Jackson was to disintegrate before him.

THE BATTLE OF MANASSAS

THE FIRST DAY, 29 AUGUST 1862

On the morning of Friday 29 August, one of Stuart's fellow cavalry officers, Captain W.W. Blackford, surveyed the aftermath of the drama that had unfolded almost on the doorstep of John Brawner's home. He recorded the Union position was "marked by the dark rows of bodies stretched out on the broomsedge field, lying just where they had fallen, with their heels on a well defined line." These men would not be the only casualties of fighting in the area. Even as Captain Blackford took stock of the previous evening's engagement, troops under Sigel and Reynolds were closing on Jackson's forces. Reynolds's Division was near Groveton, on the south side of the Warrenton Turnpike. North of the pike were Sigel's two divisions under Robert Schenck and Carl Schurz, with Robert Milroy's independent brigade further to the east, near the crossing of the Sudley Springs Road. At daylight Union troops opened the attack.

Jackson had positioned his command along a line running from Catharpin Creek, near Sudley Springs in the north to the heights above the turnpike near Groveton, facing east and south-east. Jackson's old division held the right; Ewell's Division under Alexander Dawton, Ewell having been wounded the evening before, held the center, with A.P. Hill's Division on the left. Their main line rested on the excavation of an unfinished railroad; a project started in the 1850s as the Independent Line of the Manassas Gap Railroad, but abandoned before tracks could

The land around Henry Hill had barely healed from the First Battle of Manassas, when the former foes began to make their way to this killing ground once more. USAMHI

LEFT Ten days prior to the battle, Pope's engineers completed this bridge across the North Fork of the Rappahannock in order to keep his troops on the march. USAMHI

BELOW Union forces gathered around Manassas, making use of open fields near quiet homes as they prepared for the coming fight. LC

be laid. These embankments ran in a north-easterly direction toward Sudley Mill and provided ready-made defense works for the Confederates. In front of the greater part of this old railroad were relatively thick woods, which were occupied by Southern skirmishers.

The Union forces advanced westwards, with Reynolds on the extreme left, as his Division was already the farthest west. On his right and still south of the pike, came Schenck, while on Schenck's right and just north of the pike was Milroy's Independent Brigade. Schurz's Division was north of Milroy on the far right of the Union line. The Federals advanced with spirit, their batteries shelling the woods, their skirmishers driving the enemy before them. Upon his arrival on the far left, Reynolds changed front to the north and advanced George Meade's Brigade across the pike, with the intention of turning the enemy's right. Meade's attack was inadequately supported by Schenck, however, who had detailed Julius Stahel's Brigade to assist Milroy, who was attacking the center of the Confederate line and was hard pressed. Reynolds eventually fell back some distance behind Schenck.

Meanwhile, Milroy's Brigade was pressing forward north of Warrenton Turnpike with skirmishers pushed forward beyond Groveton and Schurz's Division advancing on their right. Milroy sent two of his four regiments to support Schurz, but either through misunderstanding or perhaps as a result of getting lost, the 82nd Ohio and 5th West Virginia found themselves assaulting the center of Jackson's line. Although part of the 82nd Ohio actually managed to penetrate the Confederate line at the boundary of Lawton and Starke's divisions, a counter-attack by Trimble's Brigade soon threw them back. Further north, both Schurz's brigades, under Krzyzanowski and Schimmelfennig, were heavily engaged against Gregg's Brigade of South Carolinians. In a very aggressive defense Gregg succeeded in holding off Krzyzanowski and throwing back Schimmelfennig. After two hours of fighting, and having received no support from neighboring brigades, however, Gregg decided it was time to withdraw.

Schurz had no intention of allowing Gregg to withdraw unmolested, and around noon renewed the attack, driving the enemy through the woods. The 61st Ohio and 74th Pennsylvania of Alexander Schimmelfenning's Brigade even gained possession of a portion of the railroad embankment, holding it against repeated enemy counter-attacks, until about 2.00pm. Then the whole division was relieved by fresh troops, Hooker having been instructed by Pope to bring his, as yet unengaged, division forward. Schurz's men, exhausted and by now short of ammunition, withdrew to re-form on Dogan's Ridge.

During the morning the Union forces had acted with considerable determination, locating Jackson's line and in places even breaching it. The scene appeared set for Pope to deliver a telling blow once the rest of his army arrived on the field.

During late morning Heintzelman came up with the two divisions of Philip Kearny and Joseph Hooker, and Jesse Reno also arrived with his own and Isaac Stevens's divisions. By this time Sigel's troops, who had been marching and fighting since 5.00am, were exhausted. Expecting the co-operation of McDowell and Porter in the afternoon, Pope authorized a rest for Sigel's weary troops. As a consequence, there was a lull in the fighting until around 3.00pm, although heavy skirmishing and artillery exchanges continued.

Troopers commanded by Colonel Thorton Broadhead, who rode at the head of the 1st Michigan and 5th New York cavalry regiments, were responsible for cornering Stuart and nearly taking him prisoner. Weeks later, Broadhead was not so fortunate. After the second day of fighting at Bull Run, he was surrounded, but refused to surrender. When he would not give up, a Confederate soldier fired, striking Broadhead in the leg. The wound proved fatal. CPL

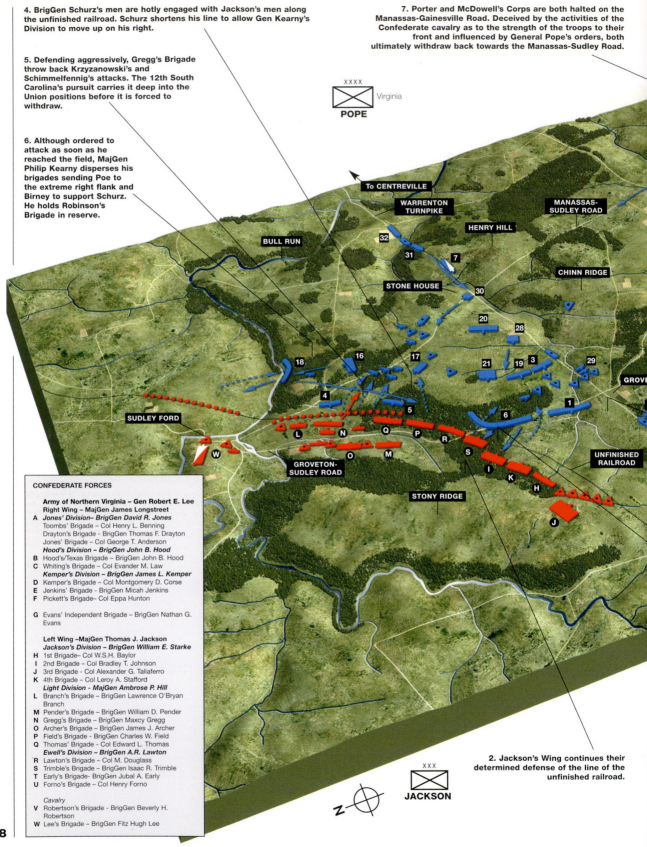

4. BrigGen Schurz's men are hotly engaged with Jackson's men along the unfinished railroad. Schurz shortens his line to allow Gen Kearny's Division to move up on his right.

5. Defending aggressively, Gregg's Brigade throw back Krzyzanowski's and Schimmelfennig's attacks. The 12th South Carolina's pursuit carries it deep into the Union positions before it is forced to withdraw.

6. Although ordered to attack as soon as he reached the field, MajGen Philip Kearny disperses his brigades sending Poe to the extreme right flank and Birney to support Schurz. He holds Robinson's Brigade in reserve.

7. Porter and McDowell's Corps are both halted on the Manassas-Gainesville Road. Deceived by the activities of the Confederate cavalry as to the strength of the troops to their front and influenced by General Pope's orders, both ultimately withdraw back towards the Manassas-Sudley Road.

XXXX Virginia
POPE

To CENTREVILLE

WARRENTON TURNPIKE

HENRY HILL

MANASSAS-SUDLEY ROAD

BULL RUN

32

31

7

CHINN RIDGE

STONE HOUSE

30

20

28

18

16

17

21

19

3

29

GROV

4

5

1

SUDLEY FORD

L

N

Q

P

R

6

S

I

K

H

UNFINISHED RAILROAD

W

O

M

GROVETON-SUDLEY ROAD

STONY RIDGE

J

2. Jackson's Wing continues their determined defense of the line of the unfinished railroad.

CONFEDERATE FORCES

Army of Northern Virginia – Gen Robert E. Lee
Right Wing – MajGen James Longstreet
A   *Jones' Division– BrigGen David R. Jones*
    Toombs' Brigade – Col Henry L. Benning
    Drayton's Brigade - BrigGen Thomas F. Drayton
    Jones' Brigade – Col George T. Anderson
    Hood's Division – BrigGen John B. Hood
B   Hood's/Texas Brigade – BrigGen John B. Hood
C   Whiting's Brigade – Col Evander M. Law
    Kemper's Division – BrigGen James L. Kemper
D   Kemper's Brigade – Col Montgomery D. Corse
E   Jenkins' Brigade - BrigGen Micah Jenkins
F   Pickett's Brigade– Col Eppa Hunton

G   Evans' Independent Brigade – BrigGen Nathan G. Evans

    Left Wing –MajGen Thomas J. Jackson
    Jackson's Division – BrigGen William E. Starke
H   1st Brigade– Col W.S.H. Baylor
I   2nd Brigade – Col Bradley T. Johnson
J   3rd Brigade - Col Alexander G. Taliaferro
K   4th Brigade – Col Leroy A. Stafford
    Light Division - MajGen Ambrose P. Hill
L   Branch's Brigade – BrigGen Lawrence O'Bryan Branch
M   Pender's Brigade – BrigGen William D. Pender
N   Gregg's Brigade – BrigGen Maxcy Gregg
O   Archer's Brigade – BrigGen James J. Archer
P   Field's Brigade – BrigGen Charles W. Field
Q   Thomas' Brigade – Col Edward L. Thomas
    Ewell's Division – BrigGen A.R. Lawton
R   Lawton's Brigade – Col M. Douglass
S   Trimble's Brigade – BrigGen Isaac R. Trimble
T   Early's Brigade- BrigGen Jubal A. Early
U   Forno's Brigade – Col Henry Forno

    Cavalry
V   Robertson's Brigade - BrigGen Beverly H. Robertson
W   Lee's Brigade – BrigGen Fitz Hugh Lee

XXX
JACKSON

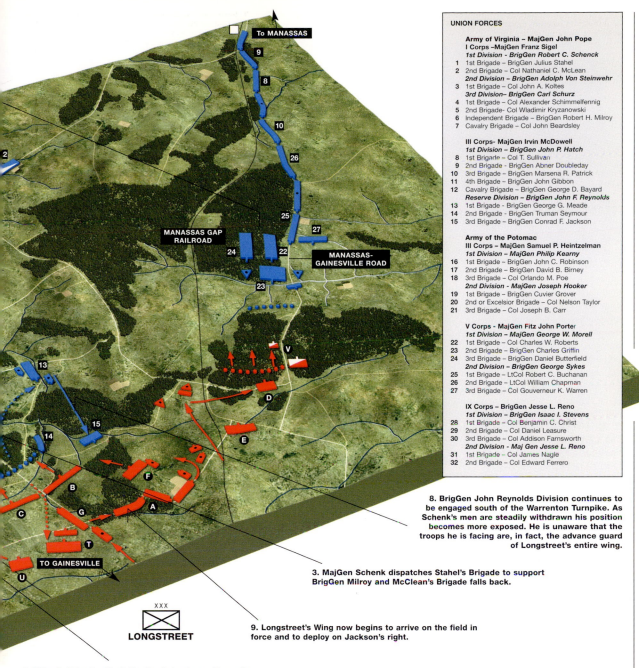

To MANASSAS

MANASSAS GAP RAILROAD

MANASSAS-GAINESVILLE ROAD

To GAINESVILLE

LONGSTREET

LEE
Northern Virginia

8. BrigGen John Reynolds Division continues to be engaged south of the Warrenton Turnpike. As Schenk's men are steadily withdrawn his position becomes more exposed. He is unaware that the troops he is facing are, in fact, the advance guard of Longstreet's entire wing.

3. MajGen Schenk dispatches Stahel's Brigade to support BrigGen Milroy and McClean's Brigade falls back.

9. Longstreet's Wing now begins to arrive on the field in force and to deploy on Jackson's right.

1. Milroy's Brigade attack the Confederate positions along the unfinished railroad but are driven back.

SECOND MANASSAS – FIRST DAY

29 August 1862, 10.00am–12.00pm, viewed from the north-west showing the Union probes against Jackson's Wing, the arrival of Longstreet's Wing and Porter and McDowell's abortive advance along the Manassas-Gainesville Road.

ABOVE **Dashing Confederate cavalier J.E.B. Stuart narrowly missed being captured on the morning of 18 August, but enemy troopers did manage to seize his plumed hat, as well as some important intelligence about Lee's plans. USAMHI**

ABOVE, RIGHT **As a preliminary to the main clash of the Union and Confederate forces at Manassas, Confederate troops raided into Union territory, striking a section of the Orange & Alexandria Railroad near Catlett's Station, on 22 August. Pope, having made his headquarters there, left behind his general's dress uniform and his dispatch book. The latter prize provided useful intelligence about the movements of the Federal Army. LC**

Pope was now confident of achieving his long-sought victory over Jackson. He was unaware that Longstreet was by now through Thoroughfare Gap, and that even now men of Brigadier General John Bell Hood's Division were arriving on Jackson's right. Indeed, the only troops Pope was expecting from that direction were McDowell's and Porter's corps, which he believed were marching from Gainesville and closing on Jackson's flank and rear at that very moment. The reality was very different. Porter and McDowell had encountered a Confederate force of indeterminate size on the Manassas–Gainesville road. Porter had halted his corps and McDowell had turned his corps around and was now marching, by way of the Manassas–Sudley road, to link up with Pope's left east of Groveton. The troops they had encountered were only six regiments of Stuart's cavalry screen, but Stuart had the 5th Virginia drag brush along the road behind them, which succeeded in convincing Porter and McDowell that they faced a formidable Confederate force. The result was that far from threatening Jackson, it was Pope's left flank that was increasingly vulnerable.

Pope's first or original report on the action, which was dated 3 September 1862, demonstrates his expectations: " ... I sent orders to McDowell to advance rapidly on our left, and attack the enemy on his flank, extending his right to meet Reynolds' left, and to Fitz John Porter to keep his right well closed on McDowell's left and to attack the enemy in flank and rear while he was pushed in front." General Pope's memory proved faulty here because he sent no such order. Around 2.00pm he did, however, order Heintzelman to organize an attack by Hooker's and Kearny's divisions. Hooker picked Cuvier Grover's Brigade to spearhead his attack, which was to be directed against the enemy's center. The brigade consisted of the 1st, 11th, and 16th Massachusetts regiments, the 2nd New

Hampshire, and the 26th Pennsylvania. After Milroy's experiences earlier in the day, Grover was convinced that the only chance of success lay in speed and impact. The resultant charge ranks as one of the most gallant and determined of the war. The men were ordered to advance slowly and steadily until they took the enemy's fire, then deliver a volley and carry the position with the bayonet without pausing to reload. The men obeyed the orders to the letter.

The 11th Massachusetts was the first to feel the sting of Rebel riflemen, but they continued the assault and pierced the Confederate line even as the 1st Massachusetts fell upon the 49th Georgia at the railroad embankment, taking the position after a brief but desperate resistance, in which bayonets and clubbed muskets were freely used. Beyond the embankment, Grover's men attacked the second line of Thomas's Brigade of Georgians and threw them back too. Grover had unexpectedly broken A.P. Hill's line. It seems almost certain that if this splendid assault had been properly supported, it would have succeeded in breaking the center of Jackson's line, but the support did not come. Indeed, Union troops under Brigadier General John B. Robinson had been so lackluster in their part of the attack that the Confederates were able to withdraw the 12th South Carolina to send against Grover. Numbers began to tell and the Southerners managed to turn Grover's left flank, throwing back his men in full retreat at the cost of 33 per cent casualties during the half hour of fighting.

What is more, Kearny's attack was to have been made simultaneously with Grover's assault, but further north against A.P. Hill's Division. Once again something went amiss. Kearny did not strike until after Grover had been driven back. When he did go into action, however, Kearny did so with great gallantry. He likewise received strong support from Stevens's Division, but all this would prove to little avail.

At first the blue-clad infantry made progress. Hill's troops had suffered greatly in all the skirmishing and fighting of the day, and ran short of ammunition. Kearny's violent, determined attack rolled up the Rebel line. It seemed as if their left was turned. In fact, under the

When Jackson's men became the unexpected guests of the Union supply depot at Manassas Junction on 26 August, they were rewarded for marching some 50 miles in two days. They found warehouses and freight cars stretching for two miles stacked with barrels of flour, biscuits, wagons, and all manner of items, including uniforms and shoes that were welcomed by Confederate soldiers, many of whom were nearly naked and went barefoot as a result of the arduous campaigning they had endured. Here Yankees survey the aftermath of this Rebel foraging party. NA

one-armed Kearny the division made it across the unfinished railroad embankment, and pushed the Southerners back to the Groveton–Sudley road (present day Route 622), the 1st South Carolina on the far left of the line falling back as Kearny's men pressed hard against the Confederate left.

Seeing his brigade begin to collapse Maxcy Gregg waved his sword furiously and shouted, "Let us die here, my men." Hill concluded that at this point victory hung in the balance, with his own troops barely able to stand this new charge. But Gregg told Hill that he would hold his position with the bayonet. Gregg was able to make good his pledge when the 37th North Carolina reinforced him at a point several hundred yards behind the railroad line, where he had managed to halt his retreating men to make a stand.

The tenacity of the soldiers was not in doubt, but the Federals were applying tremendous pressure. Fortunately for Hill, he was able to call in two brigades of Ewell's Division on his right, those of Lawton and Early. These troops hurled themselves forward and now the tide of fighting turned as the determined Confederates drove the Union infantry out of the position they had won with so much blood.

Two of Brigadier General Lawrence Branch's regiments vigorously clashed with Kearny's right, while two more of his regiments kept Hill's right from buckling long enough for 2,500 more troops under Early to arrive and stem the Union advance. The fresh fighting forces under Early not only held the line but also counter-attacked with sufficient force to halt the Yankees and drive them back.

Finally, between 5.00 and 6.00pm, McDowell arrived, bringing Rufus King's Division with him, commanded by John P. Hatch, as King was severely ill. James B. Ricketts's Division had not yet joined the fray. When Hatch came on the scene the Rebels were in the process of readjusting their line of battle after all the fighting of the day.

At that point, the seesaw struggle of that afternoon had come to a halt. The cost would prove high, Kearny having lost a quarter of his command. Despite that fact, he boasted of beating the Confederates. To some degree he was correct. Some of the Southern units, such as

LEFT **What the Confederate troops could not take, they destroyed, leaving the repair to the Federals who came in their wake. In this case the locomotive "Commodore" has been overturned. NA**

BELOW **Both sides attempted to deny the other use of vital railroad links. As such, Pope ordered equipment of the Orange & Alexandria burned when he thought it might fall into enemy hands; only wheels and metal parts remained. USAMHI**

To preclude additional raids on rolling stock, Federal troops were posted along sections of the track, such as at Pope's Run near Union Mills. NA

Gregg's Brigade, lost as much as half their number. Gregg sustained 613 officers and men killed and wounded, including all but two of the field officers in the brigade. Furthermore, ammunition had run dangerously low. Branch was aghast when he found out that after regrouping his command there were only 24 rounds remaining in his entire brigade.

Pope became convinced that the Southerners were in retreat and ready to be beaten. However, this outlook was made without knowledge as yet of Longstreet's presence, despite the fact that one of his subordinates, Irvin McDowell, realized that he faced Longstreet, but did not bother to inform Pope of this important intelligence.

In fact, during the morning of 30 August Lee had ordered Longstreet's newly arrived troops to move up on Jackson's right, where the Confederate line overlapped Pope's left, which was by this point exposed. The trap was ready to be sprung.

Longstreet recorded the situation in his official report, noting that early on 29 August his troops advanced toward Jackson. As they reached Gainesville they could hear the din of fighting so, "The march was quickened … The excitement of battle seemed to give new life and strength to our jaded men, and the head of my column soon reached a position in rear of the enemy's left flank and within easy canon shot."

At that point Longstreet deployed some of Brigadier General John Bell Hood's batteries, and placed Hood's Division either side of the Warrenton Turnpike, supported by Brigadier General Nathan Evans' independent brigade. In turn three brigades of Brigadier General Cadmus Wilcox deployed to support Longstreet's left flank and another three under James Kemper, who had been promoted to brigadier

general just a few months earlier, supported the right. Finally, Brigadier General D.R. Jones's division took up position on the Manassas Gap Railroad, "to the right and in echelon with the last three brigades," according to Longstreet's report. All this had been accomplished by around noon.

Hatch, however, knew nothing of this. Instead, he hurried along the pike toward Groveton, to press the Confederates as they tried to escape the field and, if possible, to convert this into a rout. He soon found out the state of affairs was far different from the picture in Pope's mind's eye. At about 6.30pm, at the head of three of his brigades, Hatch encountered the enemy advancing to meet him. It was a part of Hood's Division of Longstreet's Corps – Hood's Texas Brigade, and Colonel Evander Law's Brigade. The action was a sharp, costly one. In the midst of the savage brawl, Hatch supposedly sat astride his horse complacently, "while every man who approached him pitched and fell headlong before he could deliver his message." The action lasted some three-quarters of an hour, Hatch's weary men left in good order, abandoning one gun, which fell into the hands of the enemy. This gun Colonel Law indicated: "continued to fire, until my men were so near it as to have their faces burnt by its discharges."

Late in the afternoon on the extreme Union left, Reynolds undertook to renew the attack. Still in his exposed position south of Warrenton Turnpike, Reynolds was ordered to "threaten the enemy's flank and rear." At about 3.00pm he complied, although he had already voiced his concerns to Pope about the growing numbers of enemy in his path. Soon after setting out he encountered heavy Confederate artillery fire to his front, while it appeared that a considerable Southern infantry force was moving into the woods directly before him. With that, Reynolds sent Pope a courier to make known his concerns. The reply from his superior was rash and proved somewhat costly. Pope bombastically retorted, "You are excited young man; the people you see are General Porter's command taking position on the right of the

Despite Jackson's objection, Confederate Brigadier General William Booth Taliaferro assumed leadership of the Stonewall Division after Cedar Mountain. He would be wounded during the 28 August action at Groveton, NA

As sunset approached on 28 August, Brigadier General John Gibbon's Brigade braved the opening salvos of Jackson's wing at Brawner's farm. Two days later his newly blooded unit received orders to take up position along the Warrenton Turnpike east of Henry Hill, as part of the withdrawal of Union forces from the field. It was there that Major General Philip Kearny, who commanded one of Heintzelman's divisions, blurted out to his subordinate, "I suppose you appreciate the condition of affairs? It's another Bull Run, sir, it's another Bull Run!" NA

enemy." Despite Pope's complacent assurances Reynolds was forced to retire.

Pope also erred when, at about 4.00pm, he threw Colonel James Nagle's 1,500 men from Reno's Division against the woods east of the Groveton–Sudley road in another disjointed attack. Nagle's foot soldiers enthusiastically set to their task, and quickly overcame Confederate skirmishers at the outset of their advance. They pressed forward and drove off Alexander Lawton's Georgians from the railroad cut that they had occupied. Although they fell back, the Southerners did so in good order, and soon regrouped in the woods to the rear of their previous position. Jackson sent in reinforcements and with their arrival a counter-attack drove back Nagle's troops along with men of George Taylor's Excelsior Brigade, which had just come up in support of their Union comrades. Even as the Federal forces were being pressed hard, Colonel LeRoy Stafford added the weight of his brigade to the fray, and easily swept aside the Union 3rd West Virginia of Milroy's Brigade that had been sent forward to assist Nagle. At this point the center of Pope's line was in a shambles, but the commander himself had no grasp of the situation and indeed was convinced that Jackson had been bested and was even now preparing to retreat.

Thus ended the first day of the Second Battle of Manassas, which as Pope reflected in a dispatch dated 5.00am on 30 August "was fought on the identical battlefield of Bull Run, which greatly increased the enthusiasm of the men." It had been a desperate day of fighting. Pope estimated his losses at 6,000 or 8,000 men, but his estimate of the enemy's losses as twice his own was wildly out, particularly given that the Union troops were on the offense while the Confederates generally were in a superior defensive position on 29 August. On the Confederate side, however, Brigadier General Charles Field, and Colonel Henry Forno, both of A.P. Hill's Division, and Brigadier General Trimble, of "Bald Head" Ewell's Division were all severely wounded. On the Union side no general officer had been hit.

Perhaps it was this good fortune that contributed in part to Pope wrongly interpreting the action as a Union victory. While Pope's army had driven the enemy from a great deal of ground, which they held in the morning, Lee's men were far from defeated. The retirement of the enemy's line had, to a degree, been the Confederates "rolling" with Pope's punches, and were preparatory to taking the offensive the next day.

Pope completely misinterpreted the situation, as revealed in his 5.00am dispatch of 30 August, in which he gloated over his supposed triumph: "We fought a terrific battle here yesterday with the combined forces of the enemy, which lasted with continuous fury from daylight until dark, by which time the enemy was driven from the field, which we now occupy." He further related "that the enemy is retiring toward the mountains …"

Jackson had certainly taken casualties, but in the woods west of the unfinished railroad his Wing remained battle worthy. Far from preparing to retire, Jackson's men were bracing themselves for the next day's battle. In addition they had now been joined by Longstreet. Pope was aware of this, but misinterpreted it disastrously. Pope was convinced that Longstreet was directly reinforcing Jackson's line as the latter's damaged formations prepared to retire. This chimed with the picture of the battle that Pope had convinced himself was reality. In fact, Longstreet was deploying his entire Wing on Jackson's right, perfectly placed to smash into Pope's vulnerable left flank and so to roll up his line. Pope's self-delusion was to have terrible consequences on the morrow.

THE SECOND DAY, 30 AUGUST 1862

The fighting of 29 August had proved inconclusive, although at times it appeared the Union might prevail, a point Pope would make later when facing criticism for his lack of success at Manassas. Some of the blame was also placed at McClellan's door for failing to forward reinforcements from the Army of the Potomac to Pope with alacrity. Ultimately though Fitz John Porter would be made the scapegoat for the Federal disaster that was about to unfold, but his court martial was still in the future. For the moment, as 30 August opened clear and bright, Pope was confident that he was about to pursue a defeated enemy.

This was far from the case as the two armies readied to renew the match. By this point, Richard Anderson's Division had finally rejoined Longstreet, thereby negating the superior numbers Pope had enjoyed during the first day of the battle. Lee's two reinforced wings remained in their positions of the previous day, except that he had massed 36 guns, under Colonel Stephen D. Lee, on the commanding watershed in the center of his lines, where they could fire down the center of the shallow valley followed by Young's Branch and threaded by the turnpike leading through the midst of the Federal force to the stone bridge over Bull Run.

Longstreet's Corps, deployed from the center of Lee's line southward, consisted of brigades under Cadmus M. Wilcox, John B. Hood, James L. Kemper, and David R. Jones. Robert H. Anderson's 6,000 men were in reserve on the turnpike to the rear. Lee now had approximately 50,000 troops at his command in his two spread wings, the great jaws of a trap into which Pope was preparing to move, unconscious of the fate that awaited his army.

Robert E. Lee reported that after Longstreet's arrival the enemy "began to concentrate opposite Jackson's left. Colonel [J.B.] Walton placed a part of his artillery upon a commanding position between the lines of Generals Jackson and Longstreet … and engaged the enemy vigorously for several hours. Soon afterward General Stuart reported the approach of a large force from the direction of Bristoe Station, threatening Longstreet's right. The brigades under General Wilcox were sent to reinforce General Jones [Longstreet's right], but no serious attack was made …" While the battle raged on Jackson's left, "Longstreet ordered Hood and Evans to advance, but before the order could be obeyed Hood was himself attacked …"

As all this was taking place, George Sykes's Division was situated on the plateau where the Henry House stood, the site of the first battle of Bull Run. Other Federal units were nearby, when Pope noticed that the Southern skirmishers of the day before had disappeared. Again this led him to conclude that the Confederate army had been defeated, by his assaults of the previous two days and was now in full retreat, seeking safety behind the Bull Run Mountains. Wanting to cut off their supposed escape, he ordered a prompt advance along the Warrenton Road to Gainesville, and then toward the Thoroughfare Gap. In fact, far from running the rebels were spoiling for a fight and actually feared that Pope might withdraw before they could fall upon him.

While he later became known for his role in popularizing baseball, during the fight at Groveton Brigadier General Abner Doubleday had a more crucial game to play. He brought his brigade into action to support Gibbon on the evening of 28 August. NA

Union cavalry brigade commander John Buford warned that Thoroughfare Gap was vulnerable, but Pope paid little heed to this information. He sent a small force to hold the vital avenue, thereby allowing Lee and Longstreet to reach Jackson. Buford and his horse soldiers would face Lee again at Gettysburg. NA

One of Stuart's brigade commanders had followed in his uncle Robert E. Lee's footsteps. On the morning of 29 August, Brigadier General Fitzhugh Lee's troopers served as skirmishers north of Bull Run Creek. NA

John Pelham, who came to be called "The Gallant Pelham", resigned from West Point in May 1861 to head South with the intention of offering his services to the Confederacy. He served as a captain of artillery during the early part of the war, before being promoted. He still was a battery commander on 29 August, when his guns pelted Colonel Orlando Poe's 3rd Brigade of Kearny's 1st Division. NA

But he did not withdraw. Instead he called his commanders together at 8.00am near the Stone House to make final plans for the assault that he thought would defeat Lee. With this goal in mind he had brought up Porter's Corps, which had been holding the line of Dawkin's Branch, and placed it in his center. Recalling Cold Harbor, Porter did not believe, as Pope did, that Lee and Jackson had given up and were retreating, so he formed his men into a triple line of battle, across the turnpike, and placed King's Division to support his right and Reynolds's on his left. Sigel's Corps and half of Reno's was to his rear. These troop dispersals ranged into the dense forest along the turnpike and to the east of the Sudley Road. Porter was ready to advance on Lee's center. Similarly, troops under James Ricketts and Isaac Stevens reported that Jackson had not budged and was in front of them in the woods. John Reynolds also concluded that the Southerners remained in strength before him.

In fairness, Pope was not totally oblivious to the situation. Having experienced the sharp teeth of Jackson's left, he massed the whole of Samuel Heintzelman's and half of each of the corps of Irvin McDowell and Jesse Reno, to pit them against this stronghold in support of Porter's attack on the center. McDowell and Heintzelman reconnoitered the area before advancing, but they failed to detect that Jackson was waiting for them.

So it was that on the morning of 30 August, Heintzelman moved against A.P. Hill with Ricketts's Division on the assumption that his force was in no danger. This false sense of security was about to be shattered; it was just what Lee had hoped for. Pope's renewal of the engagement allowed Longstreet to pound the Union left as a diversion, while Jackson would be able to ease around the Yankee's right flank and place his wing between Pope and Washington, DC. The trap was set, and all the Rebels had to do was wait for the prey to take the bait.

Ricketts's advance was the first signal that Pope was doing just that. In short order his men had to withdraw from the hot reception they met. Reynolds's skirmishers met similarly stiff resistance, in this case from S.D. Lee's 18 artillery pieces, as they advanced to probe the enemy center. Pope finally admitted Lee had not fled but was very much present. Undaunted, he decided to press the attack. Consequently at 1.00pm he ordered Porter's two divisions along with Hatch's to make frontal attacks. Unfortunately he failed to launch any diversions or give support to this assault, thereby all but dooming the advance to failure. Interestingly enough, he did not even make any provisions for what action to take should Hatch actually carry the field.

It was 3.00pm, however, before Porter's 10,000 troops were ready to advance. Pope was finally ready to throw his entire army into the breach. From left to right were the brigades of Henry Weeks, Charles Roberts, and Hatch, while US Army regulars under Sykes formed the reserve.

The signal was given and Porter's men rushed forward, wheeling on their left. Members of Hiram Berdan's Sharpshooters in their green uniforms and carrying Sharps rifles moved out at 2.30pm, negotiating fences that ran along the Groveton–Sudley road. Before long they began skirmishing with men of Starke's Brigade, who had taken up position at a place known as The Dump. For 30 minutes they exchanged fire with their Rebel opponents, supported by two New York regiments.

Men of the 24th and 30th New York were also on the move. Holding the Federal right they withstood heavy Confederate fire. One of them recorded the savage shouts and the pandemonium as they faced their determined foe. In the process they were "transformed from the time, from a lot of good-natured boys to the most blood-thirsty demonics." The New Yorkers made it to the opposite side of the railroad embankment where their Louisiana opponents blazed away at them, ultimately driving the Northerners back down the embankment.

Roberts and Weeks fared no better, although according to one Confederate they began their advance "in magnificent style, lines as straight as an arrow, all fringed with glittering bayonets and fluttering flags." Before long though there were piles of Union bodies strewn all over the quarter-mile that lay between them and the Confederates. When they finally reached the Virginians they faced a devastating volley and were "blown away" according to one of the Southern defenders.

The dead and dying on both sides were scattered everywhere. As Porter closed in across the open field, his left was exposed to the Rebel-masked batteries. Southern shot and shell swept through his lines. Porter's attack staggered, while Longstreet opened with three batteries upon his left rear. Even then the Union men refused to give way. Jackson's troops, who had marched more than 50 miles in the past day and a half and withstood the onslaught of the previous day, were taking casualties as well. With Jackson under pressure, Lee ordered Longstreet to close in upon the Federal left. The order was superfluous because his veteran soldiers had already reached the same conclusion. Without waiting for word from their commander, they leaped forward, swinging on their left. Lee rode out in front of them as Jackson's men on the left also counter-attacked, accelerating the rout of the Federal army. The Confederate batteries soon joined in the rushing charge and were abreast of their infantry comrades all along the lines. According to one eyewitness Longstreet's gunners poured "solid shot, shell and sections" of cut up railroad track into the oncoming Federals. The results were

Orlando Poe, seen here as a brigadier general, was still a colonel when on 29 August his four regiments crossed Bull Run below Sudley Ford, placing them in Jackson's rear. This chance occurrence unleashed a hornet's nest from the Southern side that eventually caused the brigade to turn back at the "double quick" amidst a "hail of grape and canister, which ripped the sod under our feet," as a member of the 2nd Michigan Infantry, John Reuhle, recollected. NA

During the second day of the battle Lee was on the field. His presence and the arrival of Longstreet's Wing provided Jackson with the necessary reinforcements to meet the superior numbers of Union troops successfully and drive them from the field. LC

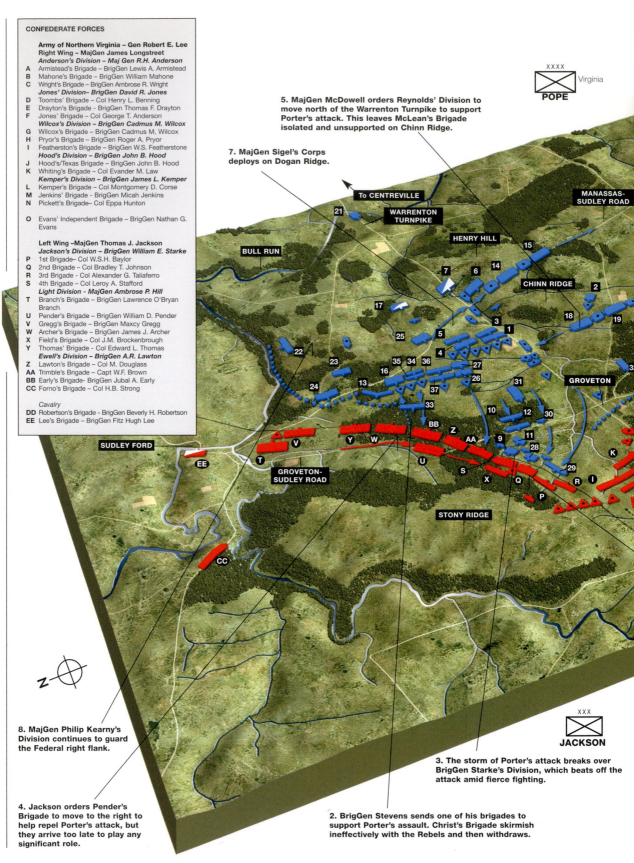

CONFEDERATE FORCES

Army of Northern Virginia – Gen Robert E. Lee
Right Wing – MajGen James Longstreet
Anderson's Division – Maj Gen R.H. Anderson
A   Armistead's Brigade – BrigGen Lewis A. Armistead
B   Mahone's Brigade – BrigGen William Mahone
C   Wright's Brigade– BrigGen Ambrose R. Wright
Jones' Division– BrigGen David R. Jones
D   Toombs' Brigade – Col Henry L. Benning
E   Drayton's Brigade - BrigGen Thomas F. Drayton
F   Jones' Brigade – Col George T. Anderson
Wilcox's Division – BrigGen Cadmus M. Wilcox
G   Wilcox's Brigade – BrigGen Cadmus M, Wilcox
H   Pryor's Brigade – BrigGen Roger A. Pryor
I   Featherston's Brigade – BrigGen W.S. Featherstone
Hood's Division – BrigGen John B. Hood
J   Hood's/Texas Brigade – BrigGen John B. Hood
K   Whiting's Brigade – Col Evander M. Law
Kemper's Division – BrigGen James L. Kemper
L   Kemper's Brigade – Col Montgomery D. Corse
M   Jenkins' Brigade - BrigGen Micah Jenkins
N   Pickett's Brigade– Col Eppa Hunton

O   Evans' Independent Brigade – BrigGen Nathan G. Evans

Left Wing –MajGen Thomas J. Jackson
Jackson's Division – BrigGen William E. Starke
P   1st Brigade– Col W.S.H. Baylor
Q   2nd Brigade – Col Bradley T. Johnson
R   3rd Brigade - Col Alexander G. Taliaferro
S   4th Brigade - Col Leroy A. Stafford
Light Division - MajGen Ambrose P. Hill
T   Branch's Brigade – BrigGen Lawrence O'Bryan Branch
U   Pender's Brigade – BrigGen William D. Pender
V   Gregg's Brigade – BrigGen Maxcy Gregg
W   Archer's Brigade – BrigGen James J. Archer
X   Field's Brigade – Col J.M. Brockenbrough
Y   Thomas' Brigade - Col Edward L. Thomas
Ewell's Division – BrigGen A.R. Lawton
Z   Lawton's Brigade – Col M. Douglass
AA Trimble's Brigade – Capt W.F. Brown
BB Early's Brigade- BrigGen Jubal A. Early
CC Forno's Brigade – Col H.B. Strong

Cavalry
DD Robertson's Brigade - BrigGen Beverly H. Robertson
EE Lee's Brigade – BrigGen Fitz Hugh Lee

5. MajGen McDowell orders Reynolds' Division to move north of the Warrenton Turnpike to support Porter's attack. This leaves McLean's Brigade isolated and unsupported on Chinn Ridge.

7. MajGen Sigel's Corps deploys on Dogan Ridge.

XXXX
POPE
Virginia

To CENTREVILLE

WARRENTON TURNPIKE

BULL RUN

HENRY HILL

CHINN RIDGE

MANASSAS-SUDLEY ROAD

SUDLEY FORD

GROVETON-SUDLEY ROAD

GROVETON

STONY RIDGE

8. MajGen Philip Kearny's Division continues to guard the Federal right flank.

XXX
JACKSON

3. The storm of Porter's attack breaks over BrigGen Starke's Division, which beats off the attack amid fierce fighting.

2. BrigGen Stevens sends one of his brigades to support Porter's assault. Christ's Brigade skirmish ineffectively with the Rebels and then withdraws.

4. Jackson orders Pender's Brigade to move to the right to help repel Porter's attack, but they arrive too late to play any significant role.

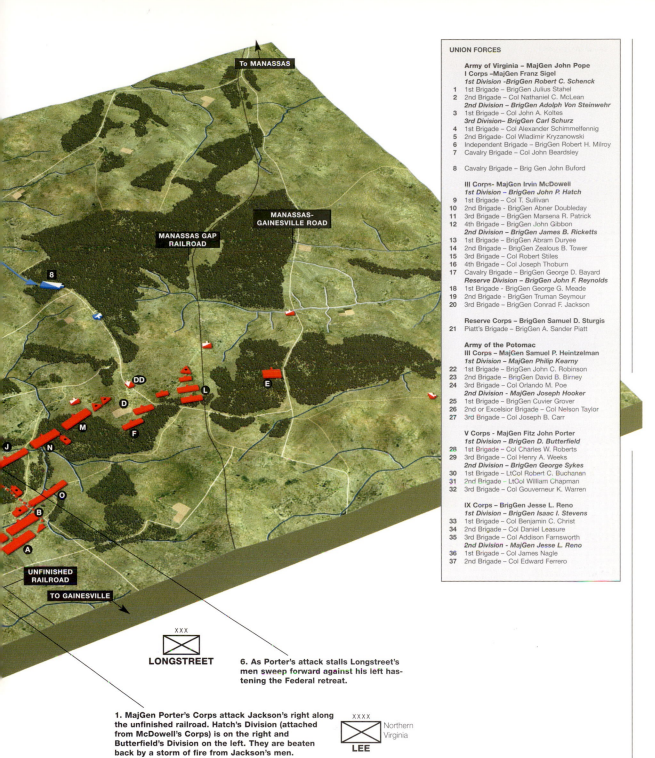

To MANASSAS

MANASSAS-
GAINESVILLE ROAD

MANASSAS GAP
RAILROAD

8

DD

L

D

E

M

F

J

N

O

B

A

UNFINISHED
RAILROAD

TO GAINESVILLE

xxx

LONGSTREET

6. As Porter's attack stalls Longstreet's men sweep forward against his left hastening the Federal retreat.

1. MajGen Porter's Corps attack Jackson's right along the unfinished railroad. Hatch's Division (attached from McDowell's Corps) is on the right and Butterfield's Division on the left. They are beaten back by a storm of fire from Jackson's men.

xxxx
Northern
Virginia
LEE

SECOND MANASSAS – SECOND DAY

30 August 1862, 3.00– 3.45pm, viewed from the north-west showing the unsuccessful attack of Porter's V Corps against Jackson's Wing behind the unfinished railroad.

Major General Fitz John Porter led V Corps of the Army of the Potomac. A veteran of both the Mexican War and the Utah Expedition under Albert Sidney Johnston, this West Pointer became a scapegoat for the Union failure at Second Manassas. Pope would have Porter relieved "for disobedience, disloyalty, and misconduct in the face of the enemy" as a reaction to the fact that he supposedly had not advanced aggressively on 29 August. Pope also faulted Porter for not succeeding in the final Union strike against the Confederates on the following day. NA

devastating, and casualties mounted as Porter threw in more troops, who at one point came on in such numbers and so bunched up that one Southern defender claimed it was "impossible to miss them." The Rebels poured on a torrential fire and as a Confederate riflemen reported, "What a slaughter of men that was."

This was more than the Yankees could bear. Although Jackson's forces were nearly at breaking point, and in the case of Stafford and Johnson's brigades, were all but out of ammunition, Porter cancelled the attack of his second line. The final blow came when Charles Field's Virginia Brigade arrived to support the beleaguered Confederate line. His unit's appearance caused Porter's troops to flee in a "disorderly rout" in masses, followed by the men of Jackson's old division from his right, who leaped across their defenses and chased them in hot pursuit. Pope's fierce attacks on Jackson's left had, in the meantime, also been repulsed. Jeb Stuart, on the right, along the old Alexandria Road, heard the famed Rebel Yell in pursuit. He rushed his brigades and batteries far in advance against the Federal left. Union General Gouverneur Warren attempted to stem the tide just east of Groveton, but at tremendous expense. Five of Hood's regiments attacked the 5th and 10th New York regiments of Warren's line. The New Yorkers deployed their skirmishers as Hood's veterans "yelling all the while" fell upon their outgunned prey. Alfred Davenport, a member of the 5th, recounted the chaos of this moment. First the recruits began to give way, then the entire regiment "broke and ran for their lives … There was no hope but in flight." As Davenport joined his fleeing comrades he "saw men dropping on all sides, canteens struck and flying to pieces, haversacks cut off, rifles knocked to pieces, it was a perfect hail of bullets."

When it was over the 5th New Yorkers in their brightly colored red and blue Zouave uniforms were in the words of one observer strewn on the ground like a "posy garden". Within ten desperate minutes of being

set upon by Hood's killing machine, the 5th New York, as historian Will Green points out, had lost more men killed "than any other regiment would lose in a single battle during the entire Civil War.

In the meantime, survivors from Porter's ill-fated attack fell back into Groveton Woods, even as Sigel's Corps and units under Milroy tried to hold fast and prevent a complete collapse on this part of the field.

Meanwhile, on the Union left, Schenck hung on to Bald Hill, but the determined Confederates swarmed upon his flank and forced him from the summit. Hood swept the line of the turnpike to the west of the Stone House. Pope's reserves, on Henry Hill, the focus of the fighting at Manassas the year before, resisted the onslaught for a time. But Jackson's left closed upon the retreating Federals toward the Stone Bridge until darkness put an end to his advance. Sigel and McDowell had fought a delaying action on Chinn Ridge but their regiments had been committed piecemeal and they were ultimately overwhelmed and forced to retire. This did, however, give Pope's demoralized brigades an opportunity to follow the crowd of fugitives that, long before the sun went down, crowded over that bridge, seeking safety behind the earthworks at Centreville and William B. Franklin's Corps, then advancing from Alexandria.

The two days at Manassas cost Pope perhaps as many as 13,824 of his men, killed, wounded, and missing. He had also lost 30 pieces of artillery and many thousands of military stores and small arms worth millions of dollars in value. This great victory at Manassas cost Lee 1,305 killed and 7,048 wounded, mostly in Jackson's command, including many fine officers.

In the wake of these losses, Pope's Army of Virginia arrived at Centreville on the evening of 30 August. Although there were many stragglers, unit cohesion remained relatively intact. General Lee's army had also suffered in these battles and, considering its very inability to

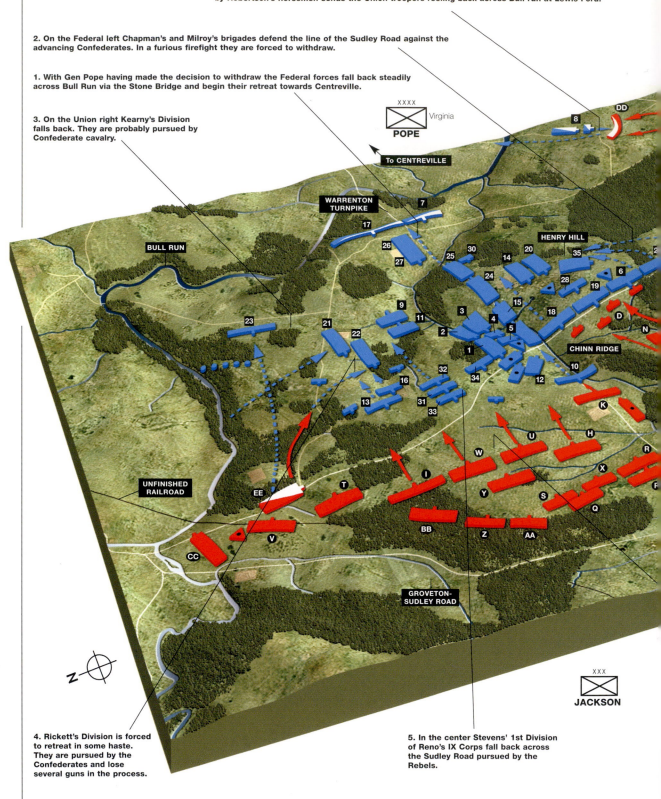

6. Buford is initially successful in his skirmishing with the Confederate cavalry but a renewed attack by Robertson's horsemen sends the Union troopers reeling back across Bull run at Lewis Ford.

2. On the Federal left Chapman's and Milroy's brigades defend the line of the Sudley Road against the advancing Confederates. In a furious firefight they are forced to withdraw.

1. With Gen Pope having made the decision to withdraw the Federal forces fall back steadily across Bull Run via the Stone Bridge and begin their retreat towards Centreville.

3. On the Union right Kearny's Division falls back. They are probably pursued by Confederate cavalry.

XXXX
Virginia
POPE

To CENTREVILLE

WARRENTON TURNPIKE

BULL RUN

HENRY HILL

CHINN RIDGE

UNFINISHED RAILROAD

GROVETON-SUDLEY ROAD

XXX
JACKSON

4. Rickett's Division is forced to retreat in some haste. They are pursued by the Confederates and lose several guns in the process.

5. In the center Stevens' 1st Division of Reno's IX Corps fall back across the Sudley Road pursued by the Rebels.

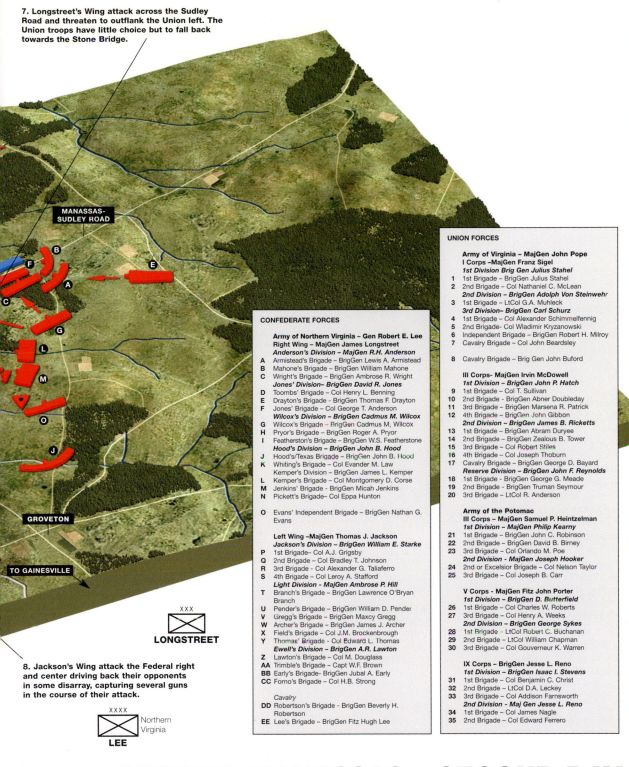

7. Longstreet's Wing attack across the Sudley Road and threaten to outflank the Union left. The Union troops have little choice but to fall back towards the Stone Bridge.

MANASSAS-SUDLEY ROAD

GROVETON

TO GAINESVILLE

XXX
LONGSTREET

8. Jackson's Wing attack the Federal right and center driving back their opponents in some disarray, capturing several guns in the course of their attack.

XXXX
Northern Virginia
LEE

CONFEDERATE FORCES

Army of Northern Virginia – Gen Robert E. Lee
Right Wing – MajGen James Longstreet
Anderson's Division – MajGen R.H. Anderson
A   Armistead's Brigade – BrigGen Lewis A. Armistead
B   Mahone's Brigade – BrigGen William Mahone
C   Wright's Brigade – BrigGen Ambrose R. Wright
Jones' Division– BrigGen David R. Jones
D   Toombs' Brigade – Col Henry L. Benning
E   Drayton's Brigade – BrigGen Thomas F. Drayton
F   Jones' Brigade – Col George T. Anderson
Wilcox's Division – BrigGen Cadmus M. Wilcox
G   Wilcox's Brigade – BrigGen Cadmus M, Wilcox
H   Pryor's Brigade – BrigGen Roger A. Pryor
I   Featherston's Brigade – BrigGen W.S. Featherstone
Hood's Division – BrigGen John B. Hood
J   Hood's/Texas Brigade – BrigGen John B. Hood
K   Whiting's Brigade – Col Evander M. Law
Kemper's Division – BrigGen James L. Kemper
L   Kemper's Brigade – Col Montgomery D. Corse
M   Jenkins' Brigade - BrigGen Micah Jenkins
N   Pickett's Brigade– Col Eppa Hunton

O   Evans' Independent Brigade – BrigGen Nathan G. Evans

Left Wing –MajGen Thomas J. Jackson
Jackson's Division – BrigGen William E. Starke
P   1st Brigade– Col A.J. Grigsby
Q   2nd Brigade – Col Bradley T. Johnson
R   3rd Brigade – Col Alexander G. Taliaferro
S   4th Brigade – Col Leroy A. Stafford
Light Division – MajGen Ambrose P. Hill
T   Branch's Brigade – BrigGen Lawrence O'Bryan Branch
U   Pender's Brigade – BrigGen William D. Pender
V   Gregg's Brigade – BrigGen Maxcy Gregg
W   Archer's Brigade – BrigGen James J. Archer
X   Field's Brigade – Col J.M. Brockenbrough
Y   Thomas' Brigade - Col Edward L. Thomas
Ewell's Division – BrigGen A.R. Lawton
Z   Lawton's Brigade – Col M. Douglass
AA Trimble's Brigade – Capt W.F. Brown
BB Early's Brigade– BrigGen Jubal A. Early
CC Forno's Brigade – Col H.B. Strong

Cavalry
DD Robertson's Brigade - BrigGen Beverly H. Robertson
EE Lee's Brigade – BrigGen Fitz Hugh Lee

UNION FORCES

Army of Virginia – MajGen John Pope
I Corps –MajGen Franz Sigel
1st Division Brig Gen Julius Stahel
1   1st Brigade – BrigGen Julius Stahel
2   2nd Brigade – Col Nathaniel C. McLean
2nd Division – BrigGen Adolph Von Steinwehr
3   1st Brigade – LtCol G.A. Muhleck
3rd Division– BrigGen Carl Schurz
4   1st Brigade – Col Alexander Schimmelfennig
5   2nd Brigade- Col Wladimir Kryzanowski
6   Independent Brigade – BrigGen Robert H. Milroy
7   Cavalry Brigade – Col John Beardsley

8   Cavalry Brigade – Brig Gen John Buford

III Corps- MajGen Irvin McDowell
1st Division – BrigGen John P. Hatch
9   1st Brigade – Col T. Sullivan
10 2nd Brigade – BrigGen Abner Doubleday
11 3rd Brigade – BrigGen Marsena R. Patrick
12 4th Brigade – BrigGen John Gibbon
2nd Division – BrigGen James B. Ricketts
13 1st Brigade – BrigGen Abram Duryee
14 2nd Brigade – BrigGen Zealous B. Tower
15 3rd Brigade – Col Robert Stiles
16 4th Brigade – Col Joseph Thoburn
17 Cavalry Brigade – BrigGen George D. Bayard
Reserve Division – BrigGen John F. Reynolds
18 1st Brigade - BrigGen George G. Meade
19 2nd Brigade – BrigGen Truman Seymour
20 3rd Brigade – LtCol R. Anderson

Army of the Potomac
III Corps – MajGen Samuel P. Heintzelman
1st Division – MajGen Philip Kearny
21 1st Brigade – BrigGen John C. Robinson
22 2nd Brigade – BrigGen David B. Birney
23 3rd Brigade – Col Orlando M. Poe
2nd Division - MajGen Joseph Hooker
24 2nd or Excelsior Brigade – Col Nelson Taylor
25 3rd Brigade – Col Joseph B. Carr

V Corps - MajGen Fitz John Porter
1st Division – BrigGen D. Butterfield
26 1st Brigade – Col Charles W. Roberts
27 3rd Brigade – Col Henry A. Weeks
2nd Division – BrigGen George Sykes
28 1st Brigade – LtCol Robert C. Buchanan
29 2nd Brigade – LtCol William Chapman
30 3rd Brigade – Col Gouverneur K. Warren

IX Corps – BrigGen Jesse L. Reno
1st Division – BrigGen Isaac I. Stevens
31 1st Brigade – Col Benjamin C. Christ
32 2nd Brigade – LtCol D.A. Leckey
33 3rd Brigade – Col Addison Farnsworth
2nd Division – Maj Gen Jesse L. Reno
34 1st Brigade – Col James Nagle
35 2nd Brigade – Col Edward Ferrero

SECOND MANASSAS – SECOND DAY

30 August 1862, 6.00– 6.45pm, viewed from the north-west showing the advance of the Army of Northern Virginia and Union forces beginning to retreat towards the Stone Bridge across Bull Run.

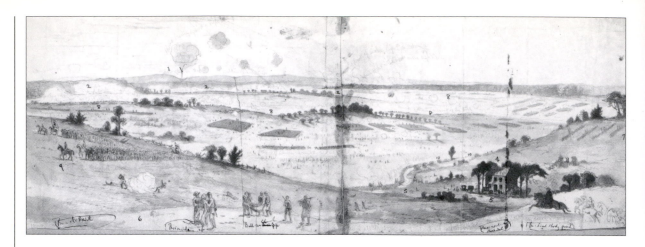

ABOVE **Newspaper artist Edwin Forbes sketched the activities of Saturday 30 August as they unfolded at around 3.30pm. From his position looking toward Groveton and north to Henry Hill from Baldface Hill he depicted: Thoroughfare Gap (1); Longstreet's line as it commenced its attack against the Union left (2); the railroad embankment that had afforded the Southerners their defense works (3); the Stone House that became a hospital (4) along with the Warrenton Turnpike to its front (5); Baldface Hill (6) and Henry Hill (7) are shown in the foreground and to the right respectively; in the distance the Federal line carries on the fight (8) as McDowell's corps move to the left flank to repel the assault (9). Finally Federal supply wagons move along Sudley Springs Road (10). LC**

ABOVE, RIGHT **The cannon that raked Porter's ranks were ably manned. Here Confederate field pieces of Stephen D. Lee's artillery battalion unleash their lethal firepower. LC**

quickly replace its losses, the Federals were, apart from their morale, in a better position than the enemy to take the offensive. Not that Pope's retreat was unwise, despite the fact that he all but apologized for it in his report. On the contrary, some critics maintained he should have placed his force behind Bull Run on the morning of 30 August. But that was a moot point.

His reputation had been heavily tarnished by the defeat at Manassas. Now his Union host was turning back to Washington, only two dozen miles away. Some alarmists feared this defeat would be followed by the capture of the capital, but this faction exaggerated the threat. General Pope summed up the situation more accurately, although with a favorable slant in his communiqué to Halleck after nightfall had ended the battle. He optimistically stated: "We have had a terrific battle again to-day." He went on to depict the engagement as a furious one that lasted "for hours without cessation, and the losses on both sides very heavy. The enemy is badly whipped, and we shall do well enough. Do not be uneasy. We will hold our own here."

Colonel David A. Weisiger, commanding officer of the 12th Virginia Infantry, also received a wound at Second Manassas, but recovered. He too went on to become a brigadier general. USAMHI

ABOVE **Union forces clung to Chinn Ridge during the afternoon of 30 August, thereby allowing Pope to establish a second defensive line at Henry Hill. At around 5.00pm Longstreet's men poured on the fire, converging on both sides of the Federal line. The pressure eventually broke the Union resolve. Pope's foot soldiers began to scatter, creating a state of "perfect bedlam", according to one of the men from the 88th Pennsylvania Infantry who witnessed the scene. LC**

BELOW **Northern troops were not the only ones to flee from Bull Run. Fearful of the consequences, these African American civilians cross the Rappahannock to follow the Federal soldiers. LC**

AFTERMATH

Unfortunately for Pope the nation was in no mood for reacting calmly and resolutely after his army had been sent packing. People saw only an uninterrupted retreat from the Rapidan to Centreville. They had watched the campaign open with his bombastic proclamation that his army was to see only the backs of its enemies, and lines of supplies and bases of communication were to be discarded. The Northern population now witnessed a retreating army before a victorious enemy after a bloody struggle. Its supplies had been captured and its communications more than once seriously threatened. They took no account whatever of the counterbalancing circumstances; they saw only what they termed results; and they were unjust to General Pope. Moreover, the strong partisanship that existed in the Army of the Potomac for McClellan rendered many, if not most, of the Peninsula officers harsh judges of their new general.

But the ordeal was not yet over. The day after the battle was rainy, rendering the fords near the turnpike impassable. Lee wanted to follow up his victory and consequently had his men on the road again in the after-noon. Jackson once more took the lead, with Longstreet not far behind.

The Southerners crossed Bull Run high up, at Sudley Ford. They then forged ahead to Little River turnpike, a fine road which ran from Aldie Gap through Fairfax Court House to Alexandria. Turning southeast they marched for Fairfax Court House, a scant seven miles east of Centreville, where they looked to strike the line of communication of the Federal army and further harass the retreat of the defeated Northern forces. The enemy surely must be demoralized and now they could strike hard again to great effect.

With this attitude, Jackson, as he did on the way to Manassas Junction, threw caution to the wind as his foot cavalry raced toward Chantilly on the afternoon of 1 September. Jackson's march had been detected by the detachments that Sumner had sent out in compliance with an order of Pope's dated 3.00am, 1 September. Stonewall left his bivouac at Sudley Ford early that morning, marched down the turnpike, and, late in the afternoon, after reaching Ox Hill, came in contact with the troops of the IX Corps under Stevens (Jesse Reno being ill) who had been ordered by General Pope across the fields between the Warrenton and the Little River turnpikes to hold the latter road, and stop the advance of the enemy toward Fairfax Court House. The Federal troops were falling back toward Germantown and Fairfax Court House. Jackson's approach on the Little River Pike had to be checked or the retreat would be jeopardized.

Stevens, though he moved with great speed and vigor, could not get to the Little River Pike in advance of the enemy. His troops encountered

ABOVE **The independently wealthy, one-armed general Philip Kearny had started his military career in the 1830s as a young dragoon officer. He was known for his bravery in combat, and was regularly at the front of the fray. Kearny's heroic manner cost him his life at the Battle of Chantilly, or Ox Hill as the Confederates referred to it, on 1 September 1862. NA**

Confederate skirmishers behind the old railroad embankment a quarter of a mile or so south of the pike. Stevens at once determined to attack with all possible energy, and the charge of his own division, numbering some 2,000 troops, proved victorious. He checked Jackson's further advance.

Stevens himself saw his men brought to a momentary halt by the terrible fire to which they were subjected in crossing the open ground in front of the enemy's positions. He seized the colors of the 79th New York Highlanders, which he had formerly commanded, and led it forward in person. This brave act cost Stevens his life.

Kearny's Division promptly supported IX Corps. The fighting was very sharp for an hour or more. During the melee Kearny, who recklessly exposed himself as usual, was also was killed.

Neither side gained an advantage. During part of the time it rained heavily, and it grew dark before the action closed. Both sides suffered considerably. For instance, the Confederates in Lawrence Branch's Brigade of Hill's Division were thrown into great disorder by flanking fire. Its commander concluded that the engagement ranked among the severest ever faced by the unit. Gregg's Brigade, which lost so many men at Manassas, again took heavy casualties. Trimble's Brigade also endured a brutal ordeal.

On the Northern side, Stevens's death denied the Union a resolute, clear-headed, able officer. When Kearny fell, he was mourned by both Northerners and Southerners as a man made for the profession of arms. In the field he was skilful, resolute, brave, and alert.

Personnel losses and the indecisive character of the engagement, which after all was only a repulse of the enemy, adversely impacted the morale of the Union Army. The Confederates outflanked the Federal right. Longstreet was up in the course of the night. On 2 September, at noon, the army being weary and the Lincoln administration under political pressure, orders came for the Union forces to hasten on to the defenses of Washington. The campaign of the army under Pope had ended ingloriously for the man who had boasted he would achieve a ringing victory for the Union. His army was soon to be disbanded.

Now the road was open for Lee to bring the war north. Lee sent forces to Harpers Ferry to snipe at the Union outposts there, but this was only a sideshow. While Lee realized an assault on Washington would be foolhardy, shifting the war away from northern Virginia and Richmond would have both strategic and psychological value. Desirous of maintaining momentum and retaining the initiative, Lee turned his victorious troops toward Maryland, a border state with mixed sympathies. An invasion there, if followed by another Confederate victory, might bring Marylanders into the Confederate cause, thereby surrounding Washington and cutting it off from direct contact with the Northern states.

More immediately, however, Lee knew he could draw his enemy a way from Confederate territory. Because Lee still sought a classic Napoleonic-style major victory, which would weaken Union resolve and perhaps lead to a negotiated peace, he pressed on into Maryland, taking the war to the North. His superiors in Richmond supported this plan to take the Army of Northern Virginia onto the offensive in Northern territory.

ABOVE **One-time Washington Territory Governor Isaac Stevens was another Union general officer who was struck down at Chantilly, Virginia. LC**

PAGES 78-79 **By the afternoon of 30 August, BrigGen William Starke's Louisiana Brigade of Jackson's Division had begun to run very low on ammunition. Then around 3.00pm the men of John Hatch's Federal Brigade advanced on the Louisiana troops who were defending a section of the unfinished railroad near the "Deep Cut". Despite heavy fire Hatch's men pressed forward. A number of the Southern infantrymen eventually ran out of cartridges and rather than stand idly by they began throwing stones at the advancing Yankees. The Confederate line was never in serious danger; Porter's attack had already spent itself and the Louisianans were speedily reinforced by C.W. Field's Brigade of Virginians. However, the symbolism of the event was too powerful to ignore and the episode became one of the most famous of the war. (Mike Adams)**

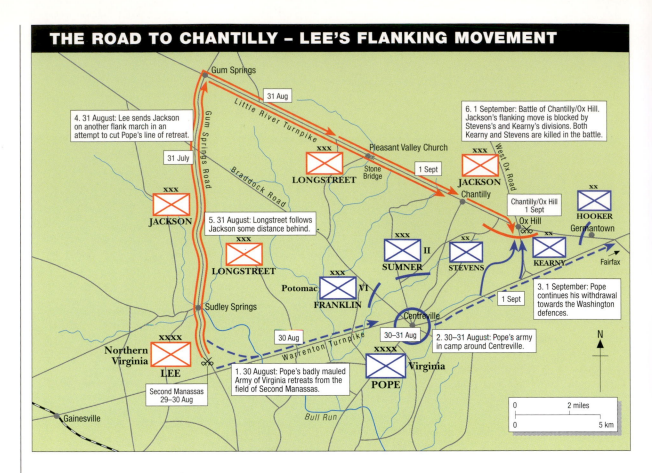

4. 31 August: Lee sends Jackson on another flank march in an attempt to cut Pope's line of retreat.

6. 1 September: Battle of Chantilly/Ox Hill. Jackson's flanking move is blocked by Stevens's and Kearny's divisions. Both Kearny and Stevens are killed in the battle.

5. 31 August: Longstreet follows Jackson some distance behind.

3. 1 September: Pope continues his withdrawal towards the Washington defences.

2. 30–31 August: Pope's army in camp around Centreville.

1. 30 August: Pope's badly mauled Army of Virginia retreats from the field of Second Manassas.

Gum Springs

31 Aug

Little River Turnpike

Pleasant Valley Church

Stone Bridge

1 Sept

31 July

Gum Springs Road

Braddock Road

LONGSTREET

JACKSON

Chantilly

Chantilly/Ox Hill 1 Sept

Ox Hill

West Ox Road

HOOKER

Germantown

JACKSON

LONGSTREET

Potomac

FRANKLIN

VI

II

SUMNER

STEVENS

KEARNY

Fairfax

1 Sept

Sudley Springs

Centreville

30–31 Aug

Northern Virginia

LEE

30 Aug

Warrenton Turnpike

Virginia

POPE

Second Manassas 29–30 Aug

Gainesville

Bull Run

N

0   2 miles
0   5 km

In less than three weeks Lee and McClellan would clash along the banks of a small Maryland creek near the town of Sharpsburg. The fighting at Second Manassas would pale in comparison to the rivers of blood that would flow at Antietam Creek. By this time, the South had complete confidence in Lee, who after Second Manassas had emerged as the pre-eminent military leader of the Confederacy. From that point forward Lee remained incommand, and for nearly three more years he was instrumental in keeping the Confederate States alive at the head of his loyal army.

Pope made his headquarters to the rear of the Stone House on 30 August. This structure has been restored to its appearance at the time of the war and forms part of the national park that interprets this battle.

THE BATTLEFIELD TODAY

In 1922, Confederate veterans and some of their decendents had the foresight to purchase 128 acres around Henry Hill. Some 16 years later the land was turned over to the United States government. By 1940, the site was dedicated as the Manassas National Battlefield Park.

Subsequently, considerable additional land was acquired, and today the National Park Service, US Department of Interior administers a 5,000-acre reserve, which because of its proximity to Washington, DC, makes it one of the most accessible of all Civil War battlegrounds. Driving from the center of the national capital, take Interstate 66 south-west for approximately 20 miles. At the junction of US 66 and US 29 there are two choices. Either continue on Interstate 66 to Virginia Route 234 (Sudley Road), using exit 47, which heads north for three-quarters of a mile to the park's Visitors Center, or take the fork of US 29, which runs south-west along the historic Warrenton Turnpike. This is the course trod by many of the combatants during the engagement. The turnpike goes past the reconstruction of the stone bridge that crossed Bull Run where the retreating Union forces withdrew on their way back to Washington. Approximately one mile west of **Stone Bridge**, on the

This monument was erected to the fallen men of the 84th New York Infantry (14th Brooklyn Militia) by their comrades after the war.

right, appears **Stone House**, the handsome two-storey former home of Henry P. Matthews and his family, which served as a hospital during both battles, and the locale of Pope's headquarters on 30 August (just to the rear of the home). The building is refurnished in period style, and is open during a portion of the summer season.

Just past the two-story residence runs Sudley Road Make a left turn on this road and proceed south for approximately a half-mile to the **Visitor Center** (turn in on the left).

The park likewise can be reached with relative ease from Dulles International Airport. Upon leaving the airport proceed to US 28 south past Chantilly to the intersection of Interstate 66. At that juncture, follow either of the two alternatives given for the route from Washington.

In all cases begin your tour at the Visitor Center. Not only is this the place where the required nominal fee (applicable to ages 17 through 61) is to be paid, but also the facility offers many useful features that will make the experience more memorable. Museum exhibits, a media presentation, and a brief battle map orientation gives background. A free color handout also concisely covers both battles. The brochure is particularly valuable in that it depicts an easy to follow, 12-mile self-guided driving tour. The book store also provides a wide range of excellent material, including audio sources and some inexpensive pamphlets that are handy references for walking tours.

Combining this latter means of exploring the site with a vehicle is an excellent way to absorb details, but be sure to wear comfortable clothing and walking shoes. Furthermore, during hot weather make sure you have drinking water. Tick repellent is also strongly suggested during certain times of the year; these insects can cause more than just an

Henry Hill, the site of the Visitors Center, offers an excellent starting point for tours of the battlefield. In the background stands the monument erected by Union veterans to commemorate the Battle of First Bull Run, a stone column that numbered among the earliest memorials to the Civil War.

irritating bite. Consult with Park Service personnel to determine if it is the season when such a precaution is advisable.

During the summer, park staff members conduct tours, as they also do on weekends for the remainder of the year, weather permitting. In addition, group tours may be arranged in advance, subject to availability. For information on this facility as well as other matters related to the site, contact the Superintendent, Manassas National Battlefield Park, 12521 Lee Highway, Manassas, VA 22109-2001, or call (703) 361 1339. Internet access is found at www.nps.gov/mana

Visitor Center hours are from 8.30am to 5.30pm daily, except Christmas. The park itself opens at sunrise and closes at sunset.

Besides the Visitor Center, Stone Bridge, and Stone House, Henry Hill also is highly recommended. The imposing statue of Thomas Jackson overlooks this vantage point where he gained his nickname during the first clash at Manassas. An easy walking path meanders over the terrain on which Porter's, Reno's, and Sigel's corps stood against Longstreet before being forced from the field on 30 August, during Second Bull Run. Information about First Bull Run also is found on this high ground. In fact, if possible, visitors should allow extra time to follow the events of both First and Second Manassas during their stay.

Other points of interest include the Unfinished Railroad, Deep Cut, the New York Monuments, Battery Heights, and Chinn Ridge. Taken together, these vestiges of the encounter help bring the battle to life.

In addition to the battlefield, the nearby Manassas Museum, 9101 Prince William St., Manassas, VA 20110, Tel.(703) 368 1873, places the military aspects of the area in local historical context. Exhibits, programs, such as Civil War re-enactors in late July and late August, and the museum store all enhance the interpretation. Visitors should also find the Conference and Visitors Bureau website at www.visitpwc.com of interest, when planning a trip to the area.

There are ample accommodations in the vicinity, many of which are more reasonably priced than lodging found closer to Washington. Restaurants and shopping are nearby as well, which while convenient have threatened to encroach on the historic scene. A picnic area north of US 29 and Sudley Road offers a good place to lunch and take in the setting.

While key reminders of Manassas remain in a setting reminiscent of 1862, the same good fortune did not befall Ox Hill (Chantilly). Except for a few acres around the two monuments erected prior to World War One, in memory of Generals Kearny and Stevens, modern structures, street lights, and other incursions have rendered the scene almost unrecognizable from its 19th-century appearance. Nevertheless, for those who are intent on completing the story of the Bull Run Campaign, proceed east from the Manassas National Battlefield on US 29 toward Centreville until it crosses Virginia 28. Take this road north until reaching US 50, then turn right and continue on for just under 5 miles to West Ox Road. Turn right and drive another 700 yds onto a residential street, where a right turn should be made. Proceed another 350 yds until coming to a small rise where the two monuments stand.

ORDERS OF BATTLE

Units present are followed by the commander's rank and name, and their estimated strength at the start of the first day of battle.

ABBREVIATIONS

Abbreviations of rank: **LtGen** – Lieutenant General, **MajGen** – Major General, **BrigGen** – Brigadier General, **Col** – Colonel, **LtCol** – Lieutenant Colonel, **Maj** – Major, **Capt** – Captain, **1stLt** – First Lieutenant

Abbreviations for types of artillery pieces are: **B** – Blakely rifle, **DBG** – Dahlgren Boat Gun, **N** – Napoleon gun, **NBH** – Navy Boat Howitzer, **W** – Wiard rifle, **6G** – 6-pdr field gun, **10H** – 10-pdr howitzer, **10PR** – 10-pdr Parrott rifle, **12H** – 12-pdr howitzer, **12R** – 12-pdr rifle; **20R** – 20-pdr rifle, **24H** – 24-pdr howitzer, **3R** – 3in. rifle.

The number before the abbreviation indicates the quantity of the pieces in that unit.

+ – type or number of gun estimated
(k) – mortally wounded or killed
(w) – wounded
* – name of commanding officer unknown

NB: Commanding officers listed are those at the outset of the battle; some subsequently were replaced as a result of wounds, death, or other reasons, during the course of the battle.

ARMY OF VIRGINIA, 29–30 AUGUST 1862

MajGen John Pope
(77,000)

Note: This figure includes those units of the Army of the Potomac assigned to Pope's command. Only certain elements of the Army of the Potomac were assigned to Pope, the majority of units remaining under McClellan's command

I CORPS

MajGen Franz Sigel
(12,500)

1ST DIVISION

BrigGen Robert C. Schenck
(3,800)

1st Brigade
BrigGen Julius Stahel
8th New York – Col Carl B. Hedterich
41st New York – LtCol Ernest W. Holmstedt
45th New York – LtCol Edward C. Wratislaw
27th Pennsylvania – Col Adolphus Bushbeck
New York Light Artillery 2nd Battery – Capt Louis Schirmer (6/10PR)

2nd Brigade
Col Nathaniel C. McLean
25th Ohio – Col William P. Richardson
55th Ohio – Col John C. Lee
73rd Ohio – Col Orland Smith
75th Ohio – Maj Robert Reilly
1st Ohio Light Artillery Battery K – 1stLt George B. Haskins (4/12H; 2/6G)

2ND DIVISION

BrigGen Adolph Von Steinwehr
(2,500)

1st Brigade
Col John A. Koltes (k)
29th New York – Col Clemens Soest (w)
68th New York – LtCol John H. Kleefisch (w)
73rd Pennsylvania – LtCol Gustave A. Muhleck

3RD DIVISION

BrigGen Carl Schurz
(2,800)

1st Brigade
BrigGen Henry Bohlen (k)
61st Ohio – Col Newton Schlech
74th Pennsylvania – Maj Franz Blessing
8th West Virginia – Capt Hedgman Black
Pennsylvania Light Artillery Battery F – Capt Robert B. Hampton
    (4/10PR)

2nd Brigade
Col Wladimir Kryzanowski
54th New York – LtCol Charles Ashby
58th New York – Maj William Henkel (w)
75th Pennsylvania – LtCol Francis Mahler (w)
2nd New York Light Artillery Battery L – Capt Jacob Roemer (6/3R)

Unattached
3rd West Virginia Cavalry Company I – Capt Jonathan Sthal
1st Ohio Light Artillery Battery I – Capt Hubert Dilger (4/12H; 2/6G)

Independent Brigade
BrigGen Robert H. Milroy
82nd Ohio – Col James Cantwell (k)
2nd West Virginia – Col George R. Latham
3rd West Virginia – Col David T. Hewes
5th West Virginia – Col John L. Zeigler
1st West Virginia Cavalry Companies C, E, and I – Maj John C. Krepps
Ohio Light Artillery 12th Battery – Capt Aaron C. Johnson (6/W)

CAVALRY BRIGADE
Col John Beardsley
1st Battalion Connecticut – Capt L.N. Middlebrook
1st Maryland – LtCol C. Wetschky
4th New York – LtCol Ferries Nazer
9th New York – Maj Charles McL. Knox
6th Ohio – Col William R. Lloyd

Reserve Artillery
Capt Franz Buell (k)
1st New York Light Artillery Battery I – Capt Michael Wiedrich (4/10PR, 2/12H)
New York Light Artillery 13th Battery – Capt Julius Dieckmann (6/10PR)
West Virginia Light Artillery Battery C – Capt Wallace Hill (6/12N)

II CORPS
MajGen Nathaniel P. Banks

Note: Not engaged in any of the main fighting with the exception of the cavalry, therefore, strengths not included except in the case of the cavalry

1ST DIVISION
BrigGen Alpheus S. Williams

1st Brigade
BrigGen Samuel W. Crawford
5th Connecticut – Capt James A. Betts
10th Maine – Col George L. Beal
28th New York – Capt William H.H. Mapes
46th Pennsylvania – LtCol James L. Selfridge

2nd Brigade
(Combined with the others)

3rd Brigade
BrigGen George H. Gordon
27th Indiana – Col Silas Colgrove
2nd Massachusetts – Col George L. Andrews.
3rd Wisconsin – Col Thomas H. Ruger

2ND DIVISION
BrigGen George S. Greene

1st Brigade
Col Charles Candy
5th Ohio – Col John H. Patrick
7th Ohio – Col William R. Creighton
29th Ohio – Capt Wilbur Stevens
66th Ohio – LtCol Eugene Powell
28th Pennsylvania – Gabriel De Korponay

2nd Brigade
Col Matthew Schlaudecker
3rd Maryland – Col David Dewitt
102nd New York – Col Thomas B. Van Buren
109th Pennsylvania – Col Henry J. Stainrook
111th Pennsylvania – Maj Thomas M. Walker
8th U. S. Infantry Battalion – Capt T. Anderson
12th U. S. Infantry Battalion – Capt T. Anderson

3rd Brigade
Col James A. Tait
3rd Delaware – William O. Redden
1st District of Columbia – LtCol Lemuek Towers
60th New York – Col William B. Goodrich
78th New York – LtCol Jonathan Austin
Purnell Legion (Maryland) – Col William J. Leonard

Artillery
Capt Clement L. Best
Maine Light Artillery 4th Battery (D) – Capt O'Neill W. Robinson (4/20R). Not on field
Maine Light Artillery 6th Battery (F) – Capt F. McGilvery (4/20R)
New York Light Artillery 10th Battery – Capt John T. Bruen (4/N). Not on field
1st New York Light Artillery Battery M – Capt George W. Cothram (6/10PR). Not on field
Pennsylvania Light Artillery Battery E – Capt Joseph M. Knap (6/10PR). Not on field
4th U.S. Artillery Battery F – 1stLt Edward D. Muhlenberg (6/3R)

Cavalry Brigade
BrigGen John Buford
(1,500)
1st Michigan – Col Thornton F. Brodhead (w)
5th New York – Col Othniel De Forest
1st Vermont – Col Charles H. Tompkins
1st West Virginia – LtCol Nathaniel P. Richmond

III CORPS
MajGen Irvin McDowell
(20,000)

1ST DIVISION
BrigGen Rufus King
(9,000)

1st Brigade
Brig Gen John P. Hatch (w)
14th New York State Militia (84th New York) – LtCol Edward B. Fowler (w)
22nd New York – Col Walter Phelps, Jr.
24th New York – Col Timothy Sullivan
30th New York – Col Edward Frisby (k)
2nd U.S. Sharpshooters – LtCol Henry A.V. Post

2nd Brigade
BrigGen Abner Doubleday
76th New York – Col William P. Wainwright
95th New York – LtCol James B. Post
56th Pennsylvania – LtCol Sullivan Hoffmann (w)

3rd Brigade
BrigGen Marsena R. Patrick
20th New York State Militia (80th New York) – Col George W. Pratt (k)
21st New York – Col William F. Rogers
23rd New York – LtCol Nirmon M. Crane
35th New York – Col Newton B. Lord

4th Brigade
BrigGen John Gibbon
19th Indiana – Col Solomon Meredith
2nd Wisconsin – Col Edgar O'Connor (k)
6th Wisconsin – Col Lysander Cutler (w)
7th Wisconsin – Col William W. Robinson (w)

Artillery
Capt Joseph B. Campbell
New Hampshire Light Artillery 1st Battery – Capt George A. Gerrish (6/N)
1st New York Light Artillery Battery L – Capt John A. Reynolds (6/3R)
1st Rhode Island Light Artillery Battery D – Capt J. Albert Monroe (6/12H)
4th U.S. Artillery Battery B – Capt Joseph B. Campbell (6/N)

2ND DIVISION
BrigGen James B. Ricketts
(9,000)

1st Brigade
BrigGen Abram Duryee
97th New York – LtCol John P. Spotford
104th New York – Maj Lewis C. Skinner
105th New York – Col Howard Carroll
107th Pennsylvania – Col Thomas F. McCoy

2nd Brigade
BrigGen Zealous B. Tower (w)
26th New York – Col William H. Christian
94th New York – Col Arian R. Root
88th Pennsylvania – LtCol Joseph A. McLean (k)
90th Pennsylvania – Col Peter Lyle

3rd Brigade
Col Robert Stiles
12th Massachusetts – Col Fletcher Webster (k)
3th Massachusetts – Col Samuel H. Leonard
9th Militia (83rd New York) – Col John W. Stiles
11th Pennsylvania – Col Richard Coulter

4th Brigade
Col Joseph Thoburn
7th Indiana – LtCol John F. Cheek
84th Pennsylvania – Col Samuel M. Bowman
110th Pennsylvania – Col William D. Lewis, Jr.
1st West Virginia – LtCol Henry P. Hubbard

Artillery
Maine Light Artillery 2nd Battery (B) – Capt J. Hall (4/20R)+
Maine Light Artillery 5th Battery (E) – Capt G.F. Leppien (4/20R)+
1st Pennsylvania Light Artillery Battery F – Capt Ezra Matthews (6/3R)
Pennsylvania Light Artillery Battery C – Capt James Thompson 4/10PR)

Cavalry Brigade
BrigGen George D. Bayard
1st Maine – Col Samuel H. Allen
1st New Jersey – LtCol Joseph Karge (w)
2nd New York – Col J. Mansfield Davies
1st Pennsylvania – Col Owen Jones
1st Rhode Island – Col A.N. Duffie

RESERVE DIVISION
BrigGen John F. Reynolds(4,700)
(Temporarily attached to III Corps)

1st Brigade
BrigGen George G. Meade
3rd Pennsylvania Reserves – Col Horatio D. Sickles
4th Pennsylvania Reserves – Col Albert L. Magilton
7th Pennsylvania Reserves – LtCol Robert M. Henderson
8th Pennsylvania – Capt William Lemon
13th Pennsylvania Reserves (lst Rifles six companies) – Col Hugh H. McNeil

2nd Brigade
BrigGen Truman Seymour
1st Pennsylvania Reserves – Col R. Biddle Roberts
2nd Pennsylvania Reserves – Col William McCandless (w)
5th Pennsylvania Reserves – Col Joseph W. Fisher
6th Pennsylvania Reserves – Col William Sinclair

3rd Brigade
BrigGen Conrad F. Jackson
9th Pennsylvania Reserves – LtCol Robert Anderson
10th Pennsylvania Reserves – Col James T. Kirk (w)
11th Pennsylvania Reserves – LtCol Samuel H. Jackson
12th Pennsylvania Reserves Col Martin D. Hardin (w)

Artillery
Capt Dunbar P. Ranson
1st Pennsylvania Light Artillery Battery A – Capt John G. Simpson (4/N)
1st Pennsylvania Light Artillery Battery B – Capt James H. Cooper (6/10PR)
1st Pennsylvania Light Artillery Battery G – Capt Mark Kerns (w) (4/10PR)
5th U.S. Artillery Battery C – Capt Dunbar R. Ransom (6/N)

Unattached
16th Indiana Battery – Capt Charles A. Naylor (6/N)
Maine Light Artillery 3rd Battery (C Pontonniers) – Capt James G. Sweet (4/20R)+
4th U.S. Artillery Battery E – Capt Joseph C. Clark, Jr. (6/10PR). Not on field during the battle

RESERVE CORPS
BrigGen Samuel D. Sturgis (800)

Piatt's Brigade
BrigGen A. Sander Piatt
(Temporarily attached to V Corps 27–31 August)
63rd Indiana Companies A, B, C, and D – LtCol John S. Williams
86th New York – Col Benjah P. Bailey

MISCELLANEOUS
1st New York Battery C (1 Section)– 1stLt S.R. James (2/N). Not on field
2nd New York Heavy Artillery – Col Gustave Waagner
11th New York Battery – Capt A.A. von Puttkammer (6/N)

ARMY OF THE POTOMAC

III CORPS
MajGen Samuel P. Heintzelman
(10,000)
5th New York Cavalry – 3 troops as escort

1ST DIVISION
MajGen Philip Kearny
(4,500)

1st Brigade
BrigGen John C. Robinson
20th Indiana – Col William L. Brown (k)
63rd Pennsylvania – Col Alexander Hays (w)
105th Pennsylvania – LtCol Calvin Craig (w)

2nd Brigade
BrigGen David B. Birney
3rd Maine –Maj Edwin Burt
4th Maine – Col Elijah Walker
1st New York – Maj Edwin Burt
38th New York – Col J.H. Hobart Ward
40th New York – Col Thomas W. Egan
101st New York – LtCol Nelson A. Gesner
57th Pennsylvania – Maj William Birney

3rd Brigade
Col Orlando M. Poe
2nd Michigan – LtCol Louis Dillman
3rd Michigan – Col S.G. Champlin (w)
5th Michigan – Capt William Wakenshaw
37th New York – Col Samuel B. Hayman
99th Pennsylvania – Col Asher S. Leidy

Artillery
1st Rhode Island Battery E – Capt George E. Randolph (4/10PR; 2/N)
1st U.S. Battery K – Capt William M. Graham (6/N)

2nd Division
MajGen Joseph Hooker
(5,500)

1st Brigade
BrigGen Cuvier Grover
1st Massachusetts – Col Robert Cowdin
11th Massachusetts – Col William Blaisdell
16th Massachusetts – Maj Gardner Banks
2nd New Hampshire – Col Gilman Marston
26th Pennsylvania – Maj Robert L. Bodine

2nd or Excelsior Brigade
Col Nelson Taylor
70th New York – Capt Charles L. Young
71st New York – LtCol Henry L. Potter (w)
72nd New York – Capt Harman J. Bliss
73rd New York – Capt Alfred A. Donalds (w)
74th New York – Maj Edward L. Price

3rd Brigade
Col Joseph B. Carr
5th New Jersey – LtCol William J. Sewell
6th New Jersey – Col Gershom Mott (w)
7th New Jersey – Col Joseph W. Revere
8th New Jersey – LtCol William Ward (w)
2nd New York – Capt Sidney W. Park
115th Pennsylvania – LtCol Robert Thompson

Artillery
Maine Light Artillery 6th Battery – Capt Freeman McGilvery (4/20R)

V CORPS
MajGen Fitz John Porter
(10,100)

1ST DIVISION
MajGen George W. Morell
(6,000)

1st Brigade
Col Charles W. Roberts
2nd Maine – Maj Daniel F. Sargent
18th Massachusetts – Capt Stephen Thomas
22nd Massachusetts – Maj Mason W. Burt
1st Michigan – Col Horace S. Roberts (k)
13th New York – Col Elisha G. Marshall
25th New York – Col Charles A. Johnson

2nd Brigade
BrigGen Charles Griffin
(Not in action)
9th Massachusetts – Col Patrick R. Guiney
32nd Massachusetts – Col Francis J. Parker
4th Michigan – Col Jonathan W. Childs
14th New York – Col James McQuade
62nd Pennsylvania – Col Jacob W. Sweitzer

3rd Brigade
BrigGen Daniel Butterfield – Commanded 1st and 3rd Brigades during 30 August
Michigan Sharpshooters Brady's Company – Capt Brady
16th Michigan – Capt Thomas J. Barry (w)
12th New York – Col Henry A. Weeks (w)
17th New York – Col Henry S. Lansing
44th New York – Col James C. Rice
83rd Pennsylvania – LtCol Hugh S. Campbell (w)

Sharpshooters
1st U.S. Sharpshooters – Col Hiram Berdan

Artillery
3rd Massachusetts Light Artillery Battery C – Capt Augustus P. Martin (6/N)
1st Rhode Island Light Artillery Battery C – Capt Richard Waterman (2/10PR; 4/N)+
5th U.S. Artillery Battery D – 1stLt Charles Hazlett (6/10PR)

2ND DIVISION
BrigGen George Sykes
(4,100)

1st Brigade
LtCol Robert C. Buchanan

3rd U.S. Infantry – Capt John D. Wilkins
4th U.S. Infantry – Capt Joseph B. Collins (w)
12th Infantry 1st Battalion – Capt Matthew M. Blunt
14th Infantry 1st Battalion – Capt John D. O'Connell (w)
14th Infantry 2nd Battalion – Capt David B. McKibbin

2nd Brigade
LtCol William Chapman
1st U.S. Infantry Company G – Capt Matthew R. Marston
2nd U.S. Infantry – Maj Charles S. Lovell
6th U.S. Infantry – Capt Levi C. Bootes
10th U.S. Infantry – Maj Charles S. Lovell
11th U.S. Infantry – Maj De Lancy Floyd-Jones
17th U.S. Infantry – Maj George L. Andrews

3rd Brigade
Col Gouverneur K. Warren
5th New York – Capt Cleveland Winslow
10th New York – Col John E. Bendix

Artillery
Capt Stephen H. Weed
1st U.S. Artillery Batteries E & G – IstLt Alanson M. Randol (4/N)
5th U.S. Artillery Battery I – Capt Stephen H. Weed (6/3R)
5th U.S. Artillery Battery K – Capt John R. Smead (k) (4/N)

VI CORPS

(Note. VI Corps, 1st Division, 1st Brigade was engaged only on
   27 August at Bull Run Bridge)

1ST DIVISION

1st Brigade – (800)
BrigGen George W. Taylor (w)
1st New Jersey – Maj William Henry, Jr.
2nd New Jersey – Col Samuel L. Buck
3rd New Jersey – Col Henry W. Brown
4th New Jersey – Capt Napoleon B. Aaronson

IX CORPS

BrigGen Jesse L. Reno
(8,000)·

1ST DIVISION

BrigGen Isaac I. Stevens
(4,000)

1st Brigade
Col Benjamin C. Christ
8th Michigan – LtCol Frank Graves
50th Pennsylvania – LtCol Thomas S. Brenholtz (w)

2nd Brigade
Col Daniel Leasure (w)
46th New York (5 Companies) – Col Rudolph Rosa (w)
100th Pennsylvania – LtCol David A. Leckey

3rd Brigade
Col Addison Farnsworth (w)
28th Massachusetts– Maj George W. Cartright (w)

79th New York – Maj William St. George Elliot (w)

Artillery
Massachusetts Light Artillery 8th Battery – Capt Asa M. Cook (6/N)
   Not on field
2nd U.S. Artillery Battery E – 1stLt Samuel N. Benjamin (4/20R)

2ND DIVISION
Maj Gen Jesse L. Reno
(4,000)

1st Brigade
Col James Nagle
2nd Maryland – LtCol J. Eugene Duryea
6th New Hampshire – Col Simon G. Griffin
48th Pennsylvania – LtCol Joshua K. Sigfried

2nd Brigade
Col Edward Ferrero
21st Massachusetts – Col William S. Clark
51st New York – LtCol Robert B. Potter
51st Pennsylvania – Col John F. Hartranft
Pennsylvania Light Artillery Battery D – Capt George W. Durell
   (4/10PR; 2/6G)

KANAWHA DIVISION (DETACHMENT)
Col W. Parker Scammon
(1,800)
(Note. The Kanawha Division was en route from West Virginia to the
   Army of Virginia and the Provisional Brigade.)

First Provisional Brigade
Col E. Parker Scammon
11th Ohio – Maj Lyman J. Jackson
12th Ohio – Col Carr B. White

Unattached
30th Ohio – LtCol Theodore Jones
36th Ohio – Col George Crook

NB: There was no cavalry in the Army of the Potomac elements

ARMY OF NORTHERN VIRGINIA, 29–30 AUGUST 1862
Gen Robert E. Lee
(55,000)

LONGSTREET'S CORPS (RIGHT WING)
MajGen James Longstreet
(27,800)

ANDERSON'S DIVISION
MajGen R.H. Anderson
(7,000)

Artillery
Maj John S. Saunders
Norfolk (Virginia) Battery – Capt Frank Huger (1/3R; 2/6G; 10PR)
Lynchburg (Virginia) Battery – Capt M.N. Moorman (2/10PR; 2/12H)
Ashland (Virginia) Battery– Capt Pichegru Woolfolk (2/6G; 2/12H)+

Armistead's Brigade
BrigGen Lewis A. Armistead
9th Virginia – Col David Goodman
14th Virginia – Col James Hodges
38th Virginia – Col Edward C. Edmonds
53rd Virginia – LtCol John Grammer
57th Virginia – Col David Dyer
5th Virginia Battalion – *

Mahone's Brigade
BrigGen William Mahone (w)
6th Virginia – Col George I. Rogers
12th Virginia – Col David Weisiger
16th Virginia – Col Charles A. Crump (k)
41st Virginia – Col William A. Parham
49th Virginia – *

Wright's Brigade
BrigGen Ambrose R. Wright
44th Alabama – LtCol Charles A. Derby (w)
3rd Georgia – Col John R. Sturgis
22nd Georgia – *
44th Georgia – *
48th Georgia – *

JONES' DIVISION
BrigGen David R. Jones
(5,200)

Toombs's Brigade
Col Henry L. Benning
2nd Georgia – LtCol William R. Holmes
15th Georgia – Col William T. Millican
7th Georgia – Maj John H. Pickett (w)
20th Georgia – Maj J.D. Waddell

Drayton's Brigade
BrigGen Thomas F. Drayton
50th Georgia – Col William R. Manning
51st Georgia – Col William M. Slaughter
15th South Carolina – *
Phillips's Georgia Legion – Col William Phillips
Goochland (Leake's) (Virginia) Battery – Capt William Turner (1/3R;
    3/12H)

Jones's Brigade
Col George T. Anderson
1st Georgia (Regulars) – Maj John D. Walker
7th Georgia – Col William T. Wilson (w)
8th Georgia – LtCol John R. Towers
9th Georgia – Col Benjamin Beck
11th Georgia – LtCol William Luffman

WILCOX'S DIVISION
BrigGen Cadmus M. Wilcox
(4,000)

Wilcox's Brigade
BrigGen Cadmus M. Wilcox
8th Alabama – Maj Hilary A. Herbert
9th Alabama – Maj J.H.J. Williams

10th Alabama – Maj John H. Caldwell
11th Alabama – Capt J.C.C. Sanders
Thomas (Virginia) Battery – Capt Edwin J. Anderson (2/10PR,
    2/12H)+

Pryor's Brigade
BrigGen Roger A. Pryor
14th Alabama – LtCol James R. Broom
5th Florida – *
8th Florida – *
3rd Virginia – Col Joseph Mayo, Jr.
Donaldsonville (Louisiana) Battery – Capt Victor Maurin (2/3R; 2 10PR;
    2/6G)

Featherston's Brigade
BrigGen W.S. Featherston
12th Mississippi – *
16th Mississippi – Col Canot Posey
9th Mississippi – *
2nd Mississippi Battalion – *
Monroe's (Dixie) (Virginia) Battery – Capt W.B. Chapman (2/3R; 2/N)

HOOD'S DIVISION
BrigGen John B. Hood
(3,800)

Hood's/Texas Brigade
BrigGen John B. Hood
18th Georgia – Col William T. Wofford
Hampton's (South Carolina) Legion – LtCol Martin W. Gary
1st Texas – LtCol P.A. Work
4th Texas – LtCol B.F. Carter
5th Texas – Col J.B. Robertson (w)

Whiting's Brigade
Col Evander M. Law
4th Alabama – LtCol O.K. McLemore
2nd Mississippi – Col P.F. Liddell
11th Mississippi – Col P.F. Liddell
6th North Carolina – Maj Robert F. Webb

Artillery
Maj Bushrod W. Frobel
German (South Carolina) Artillery – Capt W.K. Bachman (4/N)
Palmetto (South Carolina) Artillery – Capt Hugh R. Garden (1/N;
    1/12H; 2/6G)
Rowan (North Carolina) Artillery – Capt James Reilly (2/3R; 2 10PR;
    2/24H)

KEMPER'S DIVISION
BrigGen James L. Kemper
(4,000)

Kemper's Brigade
Col Montgomery D. Corse (w)
1st Virginia – LtCol F.G. Skinner (w)
7th Virginia – Col W.T. Patton (w)
11th Virginia – Maj Adam Clement
17th Virginia – LtCol Morton Mayre (w)
24th Virginia – Col William R. Terry
Loudoun (Virginia) Artillery – Capt A.L. Rogers (2/10PR; 2/12H)+

Jenkins's Brigade
BrigGen Micah Jenkins (w)
1st South Carolina (Volunteers) – Col Thomas J. Glover (k)
2nd South Carolina Rifles – Col Vinro Moore (k)
5th South Carolina – *
6th South Carolina – *
4th South Carolina Battalion – *
Palmetto (South Carolina) Sharpshooters – Col Joseph Walker
Fauquier (Virginia) Battery – Capt R.L. Stribling (1/3R; 3/N)

Pickett's Brigade
Col Eppa Hunton
8th Virginia – LtCol Norborne Berkeley
18th Virginia – Maj George C. Cabell
19th Virginia – Col James B. Strange
28th Virginia – Col Robert C. Allen
56th Virginia – Col William D. Stuart

Evans's Independent Brigade
BrigGen Nathan G. Evans
17th South Carolina – Col John H. Means (k)
18th South Carolina – Col J.M. Gadberry (k)
22nd South Carolina – Col S.D. Goodlett (w)
23rd South Carolina – Col H.L. Benbow (w)
Holcombe (South Carolina) Legion – Col P.F. Stevens
Macbeth (South Carolina) Artillery – Capt R. Boyce (4/N)

Right Wing Artillery
Washington (Louisiana) Artillery – Maj John B. Walton
1st Company – Capt Charles W. Squires (3/3R)
2nd Company – Capt J.B. Richardson (attached to Toombs) (2/12H;
    2/6G)
3rd Company – Capt M.B. Miller (4/N)
4th Company – Capt B.F. Eshleman (attached to Hunton) (2/N; 2/6G)

Lee's Battalion
Col Stephen D. Lee
Bath (Taylor's) (Virginia) Battery – Capt J.L. Eubank (1/3R; 1/12H;
    2/6G)
Bedford (Virginia) Artillery – Capt T.C. Jordan (2/3R; 1/12H; 1/6G)
Richmond (Parker's) (Virginia) Battery – Capt W.W. Parker (2/3R;
    2/12H)
Rhett's (South Carolina) Battery – 1stLt William Elliot (2/20R; 2/10PR)
Portsmouth (Grimes's) (Virginia) Battery – 1stLt Thomas J. Oakham
    (4/NBH)

JACKSON'S CORPS (LEFT WING)
MajGen Thomas J. Jackson
(24,200)

JACKSON'S DIVISION
BrigGen William B. Taliaferro (w)
(5000)

1st Brigade
Col W.S.H. Baylor (k)
2nd Virginia – LtCol Lawson Botts (k)
4th Virginia – LtCol R.D. Gardner
5th Virginia – Maj H.J. Williams
27th Virginia – Col A.J. Grigsby
33rd Virginia – Col John E. Neff (k)

2nd Brigade
Col Bradley T. Johnson
21st Virginia – Capt William A. Witcher
42nd Virginia – Capt John E. Penn
48th Virginia – 1stLt Virginius Dabney (w)
1st Virginia (Irish) Battalion – Maj John Seddon

3rd Brigade
Col Alexander G. Taliaferro
47th Alabama – Col James W. Jackson
48th Alabama – Col J.L. Sheffield
10th Virginia – LtCol S.T. Walker
23rd Virginia – Col Alexander G. Taliaferro
7th Virginia – *

4th Brigade
BrigGen William E. Starke
1st Louisiana– LtCol Nolan
2nd Louisiana – Col J.M. Williams
9th Louisiana – Col Leroy A. Stafford
10th Louisiana – LtCol William Spencer (k)
15th Louisiana – Col Edmund Pendleton
Coppen's (Louisiana) Battalion – Maj Gaston Coppen

Artillery
Maj L.M. Shumaker
2nd Baltimore (Maryland) Battery – Capt J.B. Brockenbrough (also
    known as Maryland Horse) (1/3R; 1/12H; 2/B)
Alleghany (Virginia) Battery – Capt Joseph Carpenter (2/3R;
    2/12H)
Richmond Hampden (Virginia) Battery – Capt William H. Caskie
    1/10PR; 3/6G)
Winchester (Virginia) Battery – Capt W.E. Cutshaw (2/3R; 2/12H)
First Rockbridge (Virginia) Battery – Capt William T. Pogue (2/10PR;
    2/12H)
Lynchburg (Lee's) (Virginia) Battery – Capt Charles J. Raine (3/3R;
    1/12H)
Page– Shanandoah (Virginia) Battery – Capt W.H. Rice (also known as
    the 8th Star Battery) (1/3R; 1/10PR; 1/N; 1/6G)
Danville (Schumaker's) (Virginia)Battery – Capt George W. Wooding
    (1/3R; 2/10PR; 1/N)

HILL'S LIGHT DIVISION
MajGen Ambrose P. Hill
(12,000)

Branch's Brigade
BrigGen Lawrence O'Bryan Branch
7th North Carolina – Capt Edward G. Haywood (w)
18th North Carolina – LtCol T.J. Purdie
28th North Carolina – Col James H. Lane
33rd North Carolina – Col Robert F. Hoke
37th North Carolina – Col William M. Barbour

Pender's Brigade
BrigGen William D. Pender
16th North Carolina – Capt L.W. Stowe
22nd North Carolina – Maj C.C. Cole (w)
34th North Carolina – Col Richard H. Riddick (k)
38th North Carolina – Capt John Ashford (w)

Gregg's Brigade
BrigGen Maxcy Gregg
1st South Carolina – Maj Edward McCrady (w)
1st South Carolina Rifles (Orr's Rifles)– Col J.Foster Marshall (k)
12th South Carolina – Col Dixon Barnes
13th South Carolina – Col O.E. Edwards (w)
14th South Carolina – Col Samuel McGowan (w)

Archer's Brigade
BrigGen James J. Archer
5th Alabama Battalion – Capt Thomas Bush (k)
19th Georgia – Capt F.M. Johnston
1st Tennessee (Provisional Army) – Col Peter A. Turney
7th Tennessee – Maj S.G. Shepard
14th Tennessee – Col W.A. Forbes (k)

Field's Brigade
BrigGen Charles W. Field (w)
40th Virginia – Col J.M. Brockenbrough
47th Virginia – Col Robert M. Mayo (w)
55th Virginia – Col Frank Mallory
22nd Virginia Battalion – *

Thomas's Brigade
Col Edward L. Thomas
14th Georgia – Col R.W. Folsom
35th Georgia – *
45th Georgia – Maj W.L. Grice
49th Georgia – LtCol S.M. Manning
Richmond (Purcell's) (Virginia) Battery – Capt William J. Pegram (4/N)

Artillery
LtCol Robert L. Walker
Branch (Lantham's) (North Carolina) Battery – Capt John R. Potts
    (2/12N; 2/6G)
Pee Dee (South Carolina) Battery – Capt D.G. McIntosh (1/3R; 1/N;
    2/10PR)
Fredericksburg (Virginia) Battery – Capt Carter M. Braxton (2/3R; 4/6G)
Richmond (Crenshaw's) (Virginia) Battery – Capt W.G. Crenshaw
    (1/12H; 1/N; 2/G)
Richmond (Letcher's) (Virginia) Battery – Capt Greenlee Davidson
    (1/3R; 2/N; 1/6G)
Middlesex (Fleet's) (Virginia) Battery – Capt W.B. Hardy (2/3R; 2/12N)+

EWELL'S DIVISION
MajGen Richard S. Ewell (w)
(7,200)

Lawton's Brigade
BrigGen A.R. Lawton
13th Georgia – Col C.M. Douglass
26th Georgia – Col Edmund Atkinson
31st Georgia – *
38th Georgia – *
60th Georgia – Maj T.J. Berry
61st Georgia – *

Trimble's Brigade
BrigGen Isaac R. Trimble (w)
15th Alabama – Maj A.A. Lowther
12th Georgia – Capt W.F. Brown
21st Georgia – Capt Thomas C. Glover

21st North Carolina – LtCol Sanders Fulton (k)
1st North Carolina Battalion – *

Early's Brigade
BrigGen Jubal A. Early
13th Virginia – Col James A. Walker
25th Virginia – Col George H. Smith (w)
31st Virginia – Col John F. Hoffman
44th Virginia – *
49th Virginia – Co. William Smith
52nd Virginia – *
58th Virginia – Col Samuel H. Letcher

Forno's Brigade
Col Henry Forno (w)
5th Louisiana – Maj B. Menger
6th Louisiana – Col H.B. Strong
7th Louisiana – *
8th Louisiana – Maj T.D. Lewis
14th Louisiana – Col Zebulon York

Artillery
Staunton (Balthis')(Virginia) Battery – IstLt A.W. Garber (2/6G)
Chesapeake (4th Maryland) Battery – Capt William D. Brown (1/3R;
    2 10PR)
Louisiana Guard Artillery – Capt Louis E. D'Aquin (1/10PR; 2/3R)
1st Maryland Battery – Capt William F. Dement (4/6G)
Bedford (Virginia) Battery – Capt John R. Johnson (2/3R; 1/12H; 1/6G)
Henrico (Courtney's) (Virginia) Battery – Capt James W. Latimer (2/3R; 2/N)

CAVALRY
MajGen J.E.B. Stuart
(3,000)

Hampton's Brigade – (Not present on the field)
BrigGen Wade Hampton
Cobb (Georgia) Legion – Col Thomas R.R. Cobb
1st North Carolina – *
2nd South Carolina – *
10th Virginia – *
Jeff Davis Legion – *

Robertson's Brigade
BrigGen Beverly H. Robertson
2nd Virginia – Col Thomas T. Munford
6th Virginia – Col Thomas S. Flournoy
7th Virginia – Col William E. Jones
12th Virginia – Col A.W. Harman
17th Virginia Battalion – Maj W. Patrick (w)

Lee's Brigade
BrigGen Fitz Hugh Lee
1st Virginia – Col L.T. Brien
3rd Virginia – *
4th Virginia – Col W.C. Wickham
5th Virginia – Col Thomas L. Rosser
9th Virginia – Col W.H.F. Lee

Artillery
Maj John Pelham
Ashby Horse Battery – Capt Robert P. Chew (1/B; 3/12R)
Stuart Horse Battery – 1st (Virginia) – Capt John Pelham (4/B)

BIBLIOGRAPHY

Ambrose, Stephen E. *Halleck: Lincoln's Chief of Staff* (Baton Rouge, 1962).

Boatner, Mark M. III. *The Civil War Dictionary* (New York, 1959).

Cozzen, Peter. *General John Pope: A Life for the Nation* (Urbana, 2000).

Davis, William C. (Ed.) *The Image of War Vol. II The Guns of '62* (Gettysburg, 1982).

Douglas, Henry Kyd. *I Rode With Stonewall* (Chapel Hill, 1940).

Editors of Time-Life Books. *Lee Takes Command From Seven Days to Second Bull Run* (Alexandria, 1984).

Editors of Time-Life Books. *Voices of the Civil War* (Alexandria, 1995).

Evans, Clement A. *Outline of Confederate Military History Vol III* (Atlanta, 1899).

Fishel, Edwin C. *The Secret War for the Union: The Untold Story of Military Intelligence in the Civil War* (Boston, 1996).

Gordon, George H. *History of the Campaign of the Army of Virginia, Under John Pope … from Cedar Mountain to Alexandria*, 1862 (Boston, 1880).

Greene, A. Wilson. *The Second Battle of Manassas* (Conshohocken, PA, 1995).

Griffith, Alfred H. *The Heart of Abraham Lincoln, Man of Kindness and Mercy* (Madison, 1948).

Hennessy, John J. *Return to Bull Run: The Campaign and Battle of Second Manassas* (Norman, 1999).

Hennessy, John J. *Second Manassas Battlefield Map Study*. 2nd ed. (Lynchburg, 1985).

Jensen, Leslie D. *Johnny Reb: The Uniform of the Confederate Army, 1861–1865* (London, 1996).

Johnson, Robert U., and Buel, Clarence C. *Battles and Leaders of the Civil War. Vol II* (New York, 1887).

Krick, Robert K. *Stonewall Jackson at Cedar Mountain* (Chapel Hill, 1990).

Lyon, James S. *War Sketches: from Cedar Mountain to Bull Run* (Buffalo, 1882).

Martin, David G. *The Second Bull Run Campaign July–August 1862* (Conshohocken, PA, 1997).

Polley, J.B. *A Soldier's Letters to Charming Nellie* (New York, 1908).

Ropes, John Codman. *The Army Under Pope* (New York, 1881).

Selby, John. *Stonewall Jackson as Military Commander* (New York, 1999).

Sheppard, E.W. *The Campaign in Virginia and Maryland June 26th to September 20th, 1862: Cedar Run, Manassas, and Sharpsburg* (New York, 1911).

Stackpole, Edward J. *From Cedar Mountain to Antietam* (Harrisburg, 1959).

Sutherland, Daniel E. *The Emergence of Total War* (Fort Worth, 1996).

Townsend, George Alfred. *Campaigns of a Non-Combatant* (Alexandria, 1982).

Weigley, Russell F. *Way of War: A History of United States Military Strategy and Policy* (New York, 1973).

INDEX

Figures in **bold** refer to illustrations